Between Us

C000302896

Between Us

Audiences, Affect and the In-Between

Joanne 'Bob' Whalley and Lee Miller

© Joanne 'Bob' Whalley & Lee Miller 2017

All rights reserved. No reproduction, copy or transmission of this publication may be made without written permission.

No portion of this publication may be reproduced, copied or transmitted save with written permission or in accordance with the provisions of the Copyright, Designs and Patents Act 1988, or under the terms of any licence permitting limited copying issued by the Copyright Licensing Agency, Saffron House, 6–10 Kirby Street, London EC1N 8TS.

Any person who does any unauthorized act in relation to this publication may be liable to criminal prosecution and civil claims for damages.

The authors have asserted their rights to be identified as the authors of this work in accordance with the Copyright, Designs and Patents Act 1988.

First published 2017 by

PALGRAVE

Palgrave in the UK is an imprint of Macmillan Publishers Limited, registered in England, company number 785998, of 4 Crinan Street, London, N1 9XW.

Palgrave® and Macmillan® are registered trademarks in the United States, the United Kingdom, Europe and other countries.

ISBN 978–1–137–58405–2 hardback

ISBN 978–1–137–58404–5 paperback

This book is printed on paper suitable for recycling and made from fully managed and sustained forest sources. Logging, pulping and manufacturing processes are expected to conform to the environmental regulations of the country of origin.

A catalogue record for this book is available from the British Library.

A catalog record for this book is available from the Library of Congress.

Contents

Thanks   vi
Opening   vii

Audience   1

Tasks: Audience   37

The Qualic Exchange   58

Tasks: Qualia   97

Intersubjectivity and Affective Exchange   116

Tasks: Affect   155

Closing   173
Coda   180
Bibliography   183
Index   194

Thanks

A number of people have supported the development of this book:

Thanks to all at Palgrave: your support and guidance has been invaluable.

To all the colleagues and students we have worked with, seen work with, argued with and agreed to differ from: without the generosity of your time and your thoughts, our ideas would be diminished.

Thanks to Irene and Norman for letting us clutter up your house when we needed some peace and quiet.

Particular thanks are due to Jane, John, Michael, Roberta and Victor. You are all in here somewhere, even if you can't see it.

Finally, many thanks to Robin Nelson, whose wise and kind words have shaped our thinking over the many years of knowing him.

Opening

It starts with a cheerleader, a referee and a tiger.
The tiger isn't real — it's a mascot.
Come to think of it, the cheerleader and the referee aren't real either.
They're actors.

The space is laid out like a high school gymnasium.

Actually, that's not quite true. This doesn't look anything like my school gymnasium. In fact, we didn't call it a gymnasium back then; we called it a sports hall.

It's probably more accurate to say that the space is laid out the way a high school gymnasium might look in a film. Like it would in a Hollywood film. Something from the eighties. Like *Teen Wolf*. Or maybe *The Breakfast Club*. Or maybe one of those sports films like *Friday Night Lights*. There are bleachers facing each other on either side of the court. Or pitch. Or field. No, I think I'll stick with 'court'; it's inside after all.

As soon as we file in, it is clear that the usual audience behaviours are being interrupted. We don't all walk in one direction. We make a choice, and then we all begin to peel off, some of us choosing to go to the left; others going right. Without realizing it, we are choosing sides. Literally and figuratively. I wonder who will win?

As the audience continue to make their way in, roughly equal numbers fill up both sides. To begin with, nothing much is happening. Actually, that's not quite true either. There is dance music playing. It's really loud. The tiger is doing a dance, the cheerleader is giving out popcorn. I can't remember what the referee is doing. Does she direct me to my seat? Maybe. I think she mostly stays at one end of the court with her whistle.

I think about that really loud music. It sounds good. Not good as in 'this is my kind of music' good, but good in the sense that the speakers are excellent. The sound is cranked way up, and there is no distortion. It makes me want to get up and dance. I briefly wonder if this is something I could get away with, a quick dance, but I quickly realise that this isn't quite the vibe they're going for. I wonder how I know that. How do I know that I shouldn't get up? It's not just because I have spent many years watching live performance, although that is part of it. What is it about the way the space is laid out, the way the performers talk to me, that makes me sure that while it is fine for me to talk and laugh, to turn around or wave at friends in the opposing bleachers, it is not okay for me to get up and dance?

Even though I know that I shouldn't, I still want to. I start to realise that I'm getting really excited, more excited than I would usually be at the prospect of a piece of performance. It's something to do with the way the space is being managed, and how we're being held. I want to spend more time thinking about this, but I can't. I'm too busy laughing with Nate. Nate has a really infectious laugh, and he's always very generous with it. There is a lot of talking. People are shouting across to the other bleachers. I am a tiny bit nervous, worried that we might get in trouble. But who's going to shout at us? I start to wonder if it's like this everywhere, or if the excitement (and I'm not the only one feeling it — there is something palpable in the air) is a by-product of most of the audience knowing one another.

Maybe it's because the work is being performed on a university campus, and as a result the crowd is fairly homogenised. We all know one another; at least we mostly do. Maybe that's a good thing, maybe not. But in the context of tonight, it feels right. I feel like we're the home crowd, and soon we'll be cheering for the opening pitch. Not that I have any sense what this means. These are not words that belong in my lexicon, nor are the emotions I'm experiencing. I don't do crowds, or sports, and I'm not from the United States. But I've seen enough films to recognise what's happening. Nonetheless, I'm surprised to be feeling it.

The rest of the evening goes by in a whirl. I remember doing a Mexican wave, screaming insults at the crowd sat on the opposite bleachers, desperately trying to catch a T-shirt fired from a T-shirt cannon. I didn't think that t-shirt cannons were real. I remember seeing one on *The Simpsons* once, but I thought it was a cartoon invention. And yet here I am, having one aimed at me. The T-shirt sails across the space, a cotton cannonball, I stretch out my hands and watch as Kaitlyn snatches it from the air above my head. Nate is laughing.

It's almost like I don't recognise myself; partly because the expected behaviours of the space have been interrupted, partly because I'm smiling so much that my cheeks have started to hurt.

This strange familiarity doesn't feel quite right, it's like seeing the world through foggy glass; familiar but separate.

* * *

This is a book for audiences. It is a book about audiences. It is a book for anyone who watches, is watched, and all the spaces in between.

This book is aimed at readers who watch live performance, and want to think about what is happening in the moments of exchange between the audience and the performer. With any book such as this, the concerns and the interests of the writers are going to come to the fore, and this is certainly the case here. The performance material we enjoy watching and talking about has definitely impacted upon the kind of work we have chosen to focus upon. There is a strong seam of contemporary practice being engaged with throughout this book; contemporary choreography, experimental devised theatre, live/performance art, and gallery-based film practice are all considered herein. This does not mean that we are uninterested in more traditional practices, simply that the examples we have opted to consider here better exemplify the moments of 'in-betweenness' that we aim to explore.

We have thought long and hard about whether we should offer you, the reader, any strategies for approaching this text. For the most part we have tried to think of the structure of the book as having three main sections: audience, qualia and affect. Within each of these sections are subsections; sometimes they take the form of our memories of performances; sometimes, critical writing about the ideas that interest us; and sometimes, text boxes which offer small anecdotal responses to something we have seen. The result is that there is no fixed way for you to approach the text. The interruptions of the text boxes containing the anecdotes are intended to offer some respite from the more theoretically dense writing, but they might prove to be too disrupting. If you don't like reading them alongside the longer sections of writing, just ignore them. We hope that each element stands on its own merits, so feel free to read the bits that you find useful in the order that best suits your line of enquiry. We have tried to signpost where ideas come from, so you should be able to orientate yourself and navigate back to the relevant section.

Like Matthew Goulish in his book *39 Microlectures* or Tim Etchells in *Certain Fragments*, we are working from a recognition that contemporary performance practices require different modes of spectatorship than those assumed by more traditional practices; not because the practices as somehow 'better' or 'more complex', but rather because often the work is less familiar in its structuring. The idea that the text is more open, and requires completion by the reader/audience, has been widely theorised[1] and is a perspective that has been influential on the making practices of contemporary performance. Performance-making strategies that require activation and completion are central to much of the work we have thought about in writing this book, but this is not without its own problems. Words such as 'active' and 'passive' contain value judgements that run the risk of opening up an unhelpful gap between different types of performance practice, an action that perhaps implies we are assuming some sort of hierarchy. True, we focus upon the contemporary, but this is not intended to be at the expense of other practices. Although we have built our understandings out of the types of practices we have been watching and making over the past twenty years, this is not intended to function as an exclusionary tactic. While it is true that we would consider this book to be situated within the broad project of performance studies, we still hope that it will prove to be of use to anyone who watches or makes live performance practice, whatever the genre. It is perhaps inevitable that because our own making and spectating practices tend to foreground the experiential, as authors we have a tendency to spend more time considering work that is similarly focused.

In part, this has grown out of our experience as practitioner-researchers, which is to say that much of our academic career has drawn on our tendency to understand things through action. This approach has informed our research, our performance making, our spectating and our teaching practices. This book brings together all of these concerns and as a result (hopefully) allows multiple ways in for the reader. We strongly believe that knowledge does not stop where a book does, that the arborescent low-lying branches of insight insinuate their inklings into bodies through action and 'doing'. Because you have chosen to pick this particular book up off the shelf, we assume that you are a creative being and are open to the idea that each section offers a series of performance tasks to get you thinking about audience, qualia, intimacy, proxemics, affect and so on. Sometimes these tasks will take the form of challenges – things

---

[1] Perhaps the best exemplars are Barthes and his discussion of work and text in *Image, Text, Music*, as well as his consideration of readerly/writerly texts in *S/Z*.

that we thought might be useful in thinking through the ideas we are surfacing, small offers of praxis to deepen your relationship to the material; and sometimes they take the form of more detailed embodied responses to performance practice. We also offer you a series of 'helps' – short, ludic prompts to action, broadly in the vein of Brian Eno and Peter Schmidt's *Oblique Strategies*, or a Fluxus score; something to cut out and use as a kind of playful business card. The tasks are to be interpreted in whatever way you wish, performed however you desire, to whatever audience you choose. You can do these tasks or ignore them. It is completely up to you. These tend to be solo tasks, things to do on your own, not with a group. But in this, like all things, you can ignore us; sometimes there is safety in numbers.

These tasks are for you, dear reader, for thinking about 'the 'half-way' between people and things' (Koskinen et al., 2011: 8) and are something that are done, undone, thought about, disregarded, put on the back burner, neglected, evaded, executed, ignored, taken on, wound up, accomplished, brushed off, laughed at, spat at, crapped on, looked after, made ready, scorned, spurned, fixed, destroyed, cold-shouldered, prepared, pulled off, worked, wrapped up, completed, buried, felled, seen, discounted, passed over, passed on, arranged or upended. We offer these scores to encourage thinking through doing, but also to achieve a kind of balance between process and product in the tension of the arboreal object that is the book. The tasks situated at the end of each section are a series of offerings for you to fathom. Perhaps you explore one per week, perhaps once in a blue moon. Maybe you never do them, and you just pass them on to others, these instantiations of ideas.

Similarly, how you choose to read this book is entirely up to you. Cover to cover works. Jumping through the tasks might be interesting; glancing through it lazily while you think about something else will also yield its own specific response. We should say that it feels to us very much like the kind of book you should write in. Probably in pen. Make alterations and observations as you go along. Perhaps as you add your own experiences, the 'we' can become 'us'. Just one thing – maybe don't write in it if you've only borrowed the copy. It might really annoy the next reader. But then again, maybe that is exactly the reason that you should. Offer your thoughts to the next person who will pick this book up, a sort of stretched, attenuated intersubjective exchange.

So, we believe that this is a book for audiences. It is a book about audiences. The audience is integral to any piece of performance. From this position, we begin with a simple line of enquiry: how do we watch live performance? Such a question is maddening in its seeming simplicity; the answers are manifold. How do we watch live performance? How long is a piece of string? The questions are of a similar order; it depends. The string is either as long as you cut it or as long as you find it. The way we watch live performance depends on what is being watched and who is doing the watching. In this, as in all things, context is everything.

Perhaps, then, we should reframe the question – or rather *we* should reframe the question 'How do *we* watch live performance?' The distinction is subtle, but important. The slanting script of the italics indicates a special significance afforded to the 'we' we are considering. Perhaps, then, before we can address how we/*we* watch live performance, we should consider who *we* are, in order to, if not simplify, then at least reduce the scope of the question.

We are two academics in our early forties. At least we are at the time of writing. Who knows how old we will be when you are reading this book? Maybe we will be dead. But that doesn't really matter. Whether we are alive or dead, how old we are in the moment that you hold this book in your hands and read this sentence – what matters is who the 'we' who wrote this book are. There are two of us – that's significant. One is a woman; the other is a man. We have been collaborating as research partners since the late 1990s. We undertook a joint PhD. As academics, our career has been concerned with the specifics of this 'we', and this has informed much of our research output. We are also a different kind of 'we'; we are the kind of 'we' who have been in a relationship since 1992. We married in 1996. Ordinarily in the writing of an academic book, this is the kind of information that doesn't matter; it is superfluous to the task at hand. Except in this instance, we are asking questions about 'we' in order that *we* might be able to connect to *you*; to the manifold you who might one day be using this book in relationship to audience/performer dynamics. Donald Schön wrote a significant book in 1983, a book which reminds readers that the researcher is always implicated in their research. Her body is in the archive, even if the intention is to move towards some sort of objective relationship with the material being studied. In the context of the spectatorial, there is no real way to step outside of one's subjective position, and to claim to do so is to run the risk of homogenising responses, of ossifying the 'correct' way to engage with either the generics or the specifics of a piece of performance. Which brings us to the perspective offered herein; we are writing from the perspective of a spectator. *We* are the audience. As flawed and partial as that might be, that is the only perspective from which this can be written: the specifics of our subjective viewing positions. This means the inflection of the question that opens this introduction, 'How do *we* watch live performance?', is deliberately framed.

Taking our cue from Schön, we are happy to hold our own subjective position as audience members and offer this is as one perspective of many. We hope to retain a lightness of touch, to keep our responses just that: ours. Of course, there will be inevitable missteps along the way, moments where perhaps we push the point a little too hard and find ourselves in danger of fixing down that which we hope to keep open. With this in mind, it is important that we make clear at the outset that we are not offering a 'how-to' guide. Our experience of spectating is not offered up as the model; it is not being positioned as something to emulate or attempt to replicate, because how we watch live performance depends on a range of contextual markers: How do we feel? Why are we here? What are we watching? Do we know the performers? Have we seen the work before? Are we watching this with our students? Are we watching this with our friends? Have we been fighting? Are we hungry? Are we tired? Is the seat comfortable? How warm is the theatre? Are we in a theatre? Do we have a seat? Is the man behind us coughing? Does he cover up his mouth? There are a thousand and one things that we are processing, small experiential shifts which might impact upon how we watch live performance. Some of the questions are big, existential ones. Some of the questions are small, imperceptible even in the moment of asking. These are just some of the things that inform the intersubjective exchanges happening as any of us watch live performance.

Intersubjectivity is central to this book, speaking as it does to the exchanges between people. Within this writing, perhaps the most significant act of intersubjective exchange is that which passes between the two authors. We have been thinking about the space between, collaboration co-creation for much of our adult life. Over the years we have developed lots of different ways to talk to one another. As a result, there are a lot of different voices in this book.

We've already made clear that there are only two authors, but as Gilles Deleuze and Félix Guattari wrote, 'Since each of us is several, there [is] already quite a crowd' (1988: 3). However, this isn't quite what we mean (although we mean that too). Instead, we are reflecting upon the fact that we have multiple strategies at play within the writing. The intention is not that the voices you encounter should compete with one another, but rather that we offer you, as a reader, different ways in to thinking about the experience of spectatorship. You have already encountered the word 'we' in this writing, and we have tried to explain how we intend to use this word. Sometimes authors use 'we' to address a collusion, or at least an imagined one, between the reader and the author. We have tried not to deploy 'we' in this way. There are two reasons: the first and most evident is that there are already two of us, with the writing we offer coming from two distinct subjectivities.

We have been working together for over twenty years, and we have collaborated on a wide range of research projects, some practically driven, some taking a more traditional form. The 'we' we offer is an attempt to capture the various conversations we have had over the years of our shared spectatorship. Thus, 'we' is an indication that the two of us have discussed, thought through, argued about and come to some sort of consensus about the experience of spectatorship and the theorisation of said experience contained herein. That is the obvious rationale for not using 'we' to speak of a relationship between you as readers and us as authors; simply put, it is too confusing to make 'we' do two things.

There is a further, less explicit reason. When authors use 'we' to refer to the imagined relationship between themselves and the reader, there is a danger of homogenising the experience. Thus, 'we experience x' runs the risk of foreclosing the potential for difference, and that presents real problems for us in our attempt to explore the experience of spectatorship. This is in part because 'we' can never speak to 'your' experience. In considering the generation of affective states through performance, it has become abundantly clear to us that it is difficult enough for us to speak to 'our' experience. This is not simply because there are two of us engaged in the writing of this book, although that is part of it. Mostly it comes from the increasing realisation of the impact Daniel Dennett's concept of the smearing of experience (see Section 3 on Qualia). For Dennett, this is something which impacts and informs selfhood, as our selves are developed spatially and temporally, the result of the smearing of experiences through the brain. While Dennett is offering this as a model to explain the brain chemistry at play in the development of the self, we have also begun to think of smearing as a helpful metaphor for the generation of a spectatorial self.

In our case, the smearing runs spatially, temporally and across each of our subjective positions, which is to say our experiences of watching work are informed by the conversations we have afterwards and the analysis and arguing we like to engage in. In writing this book there is further value to the metaphor of smearing; we are returning to work that we have seen over the past decade. This means we are reflecting as much on the stories we have told ourselves and one another as we are on the actual memories of the work we have seen. We rely on each other to fill in the gaps, to draw out the experience into a form that can be communicated. This further problematises the 'we' within the writing, or rather reminds us why the 'we' of this book must avowedly refer to the conjoined subjectivities from which the reflection and analysis is offered, and not assume an imagined connection to you, the reader. You will develop your own 'we' as you watch work, reflect upon work and perhaps use this to inform the creation of your own performance materials.

Or perhaps you won't.

Sorry. We're not trying to be difficult; rather, we are pausing to reflect upon another of the voices you will encounter in the writing, one that you have already encountered. Perhaps you won't develop your own 'we' because you will be working from the singular 'I', thinking and discussing from one position. The 'I' we deploy in this writing is like the 'we': not always fully trustworthy, but necessary in moments. As you make your way through the book, you might begin to notice that one of the 'I's belongs to a specific person, which is to say, 'I' might refer to something Lee has said, or 'I' might remember the way Bob described a particular moment. At these points, you might begin to feel that you can work out whose voice you are reading, who has written each particular section. It's probably best that you don't trust those assumptions.

Sometimes the writing will be singular; sometimes it will be shared. We tend to give the narrative to one or the other of us. If we are to be honest from the outset (and there is no reason not to be honest – we are amongst friends), this is a matter of expediency. Sometimes one of us writes in the voice of the other; sometimes we write from our own subject position; often we write from the double-voiced 'we'. These are all fictional positions.

We hope this helps, these introductory notes. Remember, there is no right or wrong way to engage with our ideas. As authors we certainly have ideas about what we think this book is doing, what we think this book is for. But like any book, its possibilities are infinite; we have no idea about the circumstances under which you will be reading these words. We cannot know if you are reading this section for the first time or for the fifth. We don't know anything about you.

Actually, that's not true. We know one thing . . .

This is a book for audiences. It is a book about audiences. It is a book for anyone who watches, is watched and all the situations in between.

This book is for you.

Audience

There is a running joke in our house – well, actually, it's not a joke as much as a song that gets sung in particular circumstances. In the 1969 film *Sweet Charity*, Stubby Kaye, the manager of the Dance House in which Shirley MacLaine's eponymous heroine works, sings on the evening before her nuptials 'I Love to Cry at Weddings'. Well, in our house the lyrics have been changed to 'I Love to Cry at Trailers'. This is because of Lee's unerring ability to burst into tears when confronted by a particular type of movie trailer. Usually the film is action packed, with explosions, destruction and wide-ranging peril. There comes a point in the trailer when it all just gets a little bit too much, and he begins to cry. We have always been sort of aware of these outbursts, but it came to a head when we were sitting in a cinema and a trailer for *Transformers 2: Revenge of the Fallen* started to play. If you were to watch the trailer (and why not? It's easy to find it on YouTube), you can get a sense of the destruction on offer.

It started when the first missiles hit the aircraft carrier, but really began in earnest when a single tear runs down Megan Fox's cheek. For some reason, the combination of explosions, heroics and the mild sense of peril really affected Lee, and he started to cry. Not the gentle waterworks displayed by Ms Fox, but big, wracking sobs, complete with geysers of snot. From a cold and analytical perspective, there is no sense why this would be the case. The work of Michael Bay is not famed for its opportunities for catharsis; in fact, his work tends to be dismissed as disaster porn, with an eye on spectacle over emotion. And yet . . .

This is exactly the sort of trailer guaranteed to make Lee cry. There are lots of trailers like this, but it was *Transformers 2: Revenge of the Fallen* that made us realise that there was absolutely no correlation between quality, narrative and the resultant emotion provoked.

Why this might be the case is something we have, as yet, been unable to figure out.

1

Why then do I bring this up now, at the start of an extended piece of writing designed to encourage you, dear reader, to think about the role of the audience? I think it is because tears are a strange thing. Sometimes they are infectious, sometimes inexplicable, but rarely are they unremarkable. Tears are so incredibly bound up in what is and isn't acceptable in a variety of social contexts, and they are heavily gendered. The next section, which deals with affect, considers the gendering of emotion, so know that we will consider this – just not here. I think the main reason I am reminded of Lee's *Transformer* tears is because of my own dry eyes when sitting opposite Marina Abramović for *The Artist Is Present* at the Museum of Modern Art (MoMA) in New York.

Sitting across from her was not my first 'live' experience of her practice. Prior to this, Lee and I spent the duration of *Marina Abramović Presents* (2009 – Manchester International Festival) watching her and the thirteen artists she chose to work with occupy the Whitworth Art Gallery for eighteen days. After our engagement with *The Artist Is Present,* we returned to her work, visiting *The Life and Death of Marina Abramović* and *11 Rooms* (both 2011 – Manchester International Festival) and *512 Hours* (2014 – Serpentine Gallery, London). Although questions of our spectatorship were raised, and specifically what was being asked of us in all of these pieces, it was *The Artist Is Present* that crystallised something of the performer/audience exchange and therefore the work that has exercised us the most.

Perhaps it was the fact that *The Artist Is Present* was positioned as 'a new elaboration on her landmark durational work with Ulay' (Giannachi, Kaye and Shanks, 2012: 21) that peaked our interest; certainly *Nightsea Crossing* has been the subject of great many articles and op-ed pieces, and arguably both pieces have been over-theorised within the broader context of presence, absence and issues of spectatorship. As a result, perhaps our visit to MoMA was overburdened with expectation.

As I begin to reflect here on the experience, I worry whether another account of an already over-theorised piece is entirely necessary. I am anxious that the addition of my voice to the existing clamour around *The Artist Is Present* will simply reinforce the sense that this is a piece designed to be written about, and that much like the ouroboros, it is eating its own tail. I'm not certain how much I want to be involved in making such a meal. However, I am emboldened by the observation made by Patrice Pavis, who reminds me that

> [t]he work, once performed, disappears for ever. The only memory which one can preserve is that of the spectator's more or less distracted perception. (1992: 67)

And this is what I can offer. My 'distracted perception' is filtered by the specifics of my singular expectations, life experiences and concerns. Certainly, my experience differs vastly from Lee's. He spent the whole time sitting opposite Abramović counting, worried that he was taking too long, informed by the snarky comments of the security guard who stood at the head of the queue, monitoring behaviour and explaining the rules of engagement. I heard no such comment and was unconcerned that my forty-two minutes was too long an encounter. Ultimately, I have decided that it is fine for me to offer my account precisely because it is mine and no one else's. If memory alone can preserve the experience of the spectator, then perhaps capturing my experience goes some way towards offering a way into a performance to those who weren't able to be in the room with it.

Taking up Pavis's claim for disappearance is Peggy Phelan, who reminds her reader that the 'only life [of performance] is in the present (1993: 146). This, in turn, led to a counter from Philip Auslander and a resulting two decades of back and forth, with two further significant edited texts being published in this field over the past two years. I'm not trying to contribute here, just recognising that inevitably any account of a thing now past will be subsumed by the wider debates. Given that this project by Abramović has been somewhat traduced, it might appear that my late addition is in some way commenting upon recent scholarship. For example, Amelia Jones suggests that

> *The Artist Is Present* exemplified the politically dangerous trend towards reifying precisely that which is still being claimed as 'authentic' in its supposed transfer of unmediated emotions and energy. In short, *The Artist Is Present* exemplifies what is lost when performance is institutionalised, objectified, and, by extension, commodified under the guise of somehow capturing the ephemeral. You can't 'curate', plan in advance, or otherwise present 'presence'; it is something that happens of its own accord through interpersonal encounters. (Jones, 2012: 160)

This critique is fascinating, but not part of the landscape of my memory. My thoughts, and those that follow, are less concerned with conversations around curatorship and the institutionalisation of art than they are with the experience of the exchange. I intend to offer my 'more or less distracted perception' as a means to move in towards a consideration of what might open up between a performer and a spectator, which is in itself a significant enough place to begin.

Sitting opposite Abramović in the atrium space of New York's MoMA was a disconcerting experience. My memory doesn't begin at the table, but in the queue beforehand. Joining the queue offers no guarantee of an audience with Abramović. Depending on which of the seventy days of Abramović's installation attended would impact heavily upon waiting times, but even then those hoping to sit opposite her were at the mercy of the people further ahead in the queue. Initially, there were no time constraints placed upon those who chose to sit opposite. Audience members were advised that they could stay as long as they felt that the 'conversation' was ongoing. In practice, as long as eye contact was held, the conversation was considered 'live'.

There are six floors to MoMA, with the Marron Atrium occupying the second floor and visible from floors two through six. Abramović's installation of *The Artist Is Present* filled the atrium for seventy days, and as a result the potential for engagement with the piece was multilayered. Anyone entering the gallery and visiting any of the various galleries would have seen the work. This first level of engagement might be compared to the 'accidental' audience as defined by Schechner, an audience who are unfamiliar with the content and circumstances of the material, and thus come to the work without preconceptions. In the case of *The Artist Is Present,* this might not translate into a focused engagement, with the work potentially functioning as little more than background noise. The layout of the space was such that the floor of the atrium had a clear demarcation of what was considered to be the performance area. Those accessing the galleries surrounding the atrium had to navigate the reduced floor space and skirt the edge of the queue waiting for their turn in front of Abramović.

There was, of course, the possibility that those accessing the galleries might shift from an accidental engagement to a more intentional relationship to the work. Those queuing form a second level of audience, an audience that made the decision to engage with the work. By queuing they were showing a commitment to the piece, especially as there was no guarantee that by joining the queue they would find themselves opposite Abramović. The third level of audience is made up of those who made it from the queue and found themselves sitting opposite Abramović. Further to this were those who watched MoMA's live stream of the event.

I'm aware that I am forestalling the telling of my story, resisting letting you in on what it was like to sit opposite her, fully aware of the pregnancy of all the many levels of gaze present at the event. This isn't because I am trying to eke out as much from the experience as possible. I think it's because I'm a little bit embarrassed, somewhat ashamed. Or maybe I've just talked this all over with Lee too many times, and really I'm holding his anxiety in my body. But I promise, I am getting there.

The egalitarian nature of queuing gave the impression that all comers were meeting the work in relative equality. Of course, as with any such public event, the process was rigorously stage-managed, with celebrities and friends being brought to the front of the queue shortly before the opening of the gallery. But even with this fast tracking, once the doors were open, there was no way to exit the space without negotiating the crowds. Full disclosure: Lee and I jumped the queue. We had worked on a previous project with an assistant to Abramović, and in the process of trying to organise a coffee with him, he invited us to join the queue early one morning. We arrived half an hour before the gallery opened. At that point the foyer was full of people checking coats and bags, buying tickets and milling around, awaiting the opening proper. We stood in a crowd of about three hundred, watching the stairs to the atrium. Just before 10 A.M., Davide came to the top of the stairs and waved us up. Perhaps this was the first moment that I became fully aware of the weight of the gaze. Perhaps we were asking for it. We manoeuvred our way through the crowd and made our way up the stairs to join a group of four other people waiting. They were ahead of us in this pre-queue. All friends of Abramović, they were engaged in conversation but stopped to pass some brief pleasantries. We were all led into the atrium and brought to the area which had been designated as the entrance to the performance space. We were fifth and sixth in the queue as the rest of the public ran in, jockeying to be as near to the front as possible.

Evidently we felt a certain level of awkwardness as others filed in behind us. Questions were asked of the museum guards, along the lines of 'What makes them so special?', questions that the guards had little patience in offering a response to, perhaps equally irritated by the apparent subversion of the rules. Although we don't wish to dwell on that initial awkwardness, it would be disingenuous not to mention the circumstances of our initial arrival. It informed the subjective position we occupied and impacted significantly upon Lee's ability to engage with the work. That being said, any perceived elevation to special status was momentary, primarily because it was a distinction that didn't last.

My experience was marked by a certain amount of intersubjective leaking, an experience that occurred as a result of following on directly from three people known to Abramović. It was this odd bleed over that reminded me of Lee's *Transformer* tears, but I'll come to that. The four people in the queue before me all knew Abramović, and as the time passed and each subsequent person sat in front of her, she became more and more visibly upset. By the time I sat down opposite her, she was crying freely. In the aftermath of *The Artist Is Present*, much has been made of the tears of the sitters, but less of Abramović's tears. Sitting opposite her, watching her cry, was a curiously disconnecting experience. Sitting across from a woman who was struggling with her emotions, knowing that she was less than an hour into her day-long engagement, a day that was just one in a sea of seventy other such days, was deeply affecting. I felt for her — how could I not? Tears do that. I wanted to somehow be there for her in this struggle, to know that she was held.

And yet ...

There was still that disconnect. I was fully aware that these tears were not for me. This emotion was not part of an intersubjective moment in which I was being witnessed; I was not being seen by this woman. In fact, it felt very much as if the opposite was the case. I was merely a quiet observer of her turmoil, experiencing something that was totally unconnected to my presence. Of course, it is hard to reflect upon this lacuna without sounding like I am complaining that I didn't get my money's worth; that I was somehow short-changed. I run the risk of sounding as though I understand the work only in the context of transaction. I have thought a lot about this, and I hope that this is not the case. Instead, my response was largely one of confusion. The script I had been offered by the security guard, in advance of sitting, was that I should imagine my exchange with Abramović as a silent conversation, that it was 'live' as long as I remained engaged. But being the recipient of tears intended for another sitter somehow undermined the much-repeated claim that Abramović was involved in a silent communion with each individual who sat opposite her.

When reflecting upon the experience, it is difficult not to move straight towards the critique and to foreground the analytic, but I want to try to stay with my experience. At first, I thought perhaps my experience of holding Abramović's empty gaze was an opportunity to reflect upon absence and presence in performance as I felt myself fade before her. I was reminded of Schneider, who suggests that

> [i]f we consider performance as 'of' disappearance, if we think of the ephemeral as that which 'vanishes', and if we think of performance as the antithesis of preservation, do we limit ourselves to an understanding of performance predetermined by a cultural habituation to the patrilineal, west-identified (arguably white-cultural) logic of the archive? (Schneider, 2012: 63)

But this is the wrong order of absence and presence; Schneider is offering a debate on the ability to abide versus the ability to disappear. It is caught up with a critique of the commercialisation of arts practice, and for me to get caught in a consideration of this is to occlude questions around *my* presence, and *my* perception of Abramović's absence. As I felt myself disappearing, I wondered what it meant to be present in performance – not as a performer, but as an audience member. What is interesting, at an analytical, but also at an emotional level, is that I experienced an absence in exactly the moment I was supposed to be experiencing presence. To be clear, I am not interested in framing this within the landscape of failure; I don't intend to suggest that my experience of *The Artist Is Present* invalidates the experiences of others. I don't even wish to position the specifics of *my* engagement as somehow failed.

As I stated above, the rhetoric offered by the museum guard in the moments before I sat across from Abramović was to position the exchange as a conversation without words. I was reminded to maintain eye contact throughout because to break eye contact is to signal that the conversation is over. I was reminded that it wasn't a staring contest (although it had been reduced to such in a variety of media reports), but rather an opportunity to really 'be' with someone. Thus, my experience, with Abramović crying and lowering her head to the table three times in the early minutes of our engagement, deviated immediately from the script I had just been prepared with. On a personal level (for how else am I to respond?), I wondered what exactly I should make of these glances away. At first I wondered if they were they an invitation to leave, after all I had just been reminded that to look away is to end the conversation. Were these rules also applicable to Abramović? I didn't think so, and so I stayed, waiting to find some way to assert my own voice within this conversation.

The result was that I set myself a very simple task. I would stay at the table and continue to hold her gaze until the moment I felt that I was seen. I have thought a lot about this decision since, worrying that perhaps it sprang from some petty desire to be important. I don't think that this was the case; rather, I believe that I was to trying to find some way to honour the idea of presence, of being present.

My experience was one of a slow coming into focus. At the start of my time at the table, I was witness to a woman who wasn't there. Actually, I think I need to be clearer here; I am not suggesting that Abramović was not engaged; there was no sense that she was 'phoning it in'. Rather, it felt to me as though she couldn't initially find her way to the table to 'meet' me. In terms of emotional exchange, I felt the weight of this absence at the outset, followed by a slow presencing as we made our way towards one another. I think that my initial desire to hold her in some way, to be there for this crying stranger, was what kept me at the table. I think this is where Lee's *Transformer* tears come back. Those four friends, one after another, were like the explosions, the cars becoming robots, the soft focus distress of Megan Fox; they were simply too much to hold in one body in such a short time. Lee has seen *Transformers 2: Rise of the Fallen* all the way through. He remained dry-eyed throughout. There was nothing in the film as it played out in real time that moved him; it was merely another opportunity to sell tickets and toys, as calculated as one might expect. The tears of Abramović were not for me, but crucially they were not for her friends. Or at least I don't think they were *just* for her friends. They were the inevitable result of too much sensory input, an overloading of intersubjective exchange, resulting in a clouding of the 'real' moment – I wish I could think of a way to say that without recourse to the word 'real', but I'm at a loss. That her tears were misplaced, or perhaps a misdirection, does nothing to reduce their impact on the audience watching our exchange, any more than they reduce the impact of all those tears shed by those who had, and who would, sit in the chair I occupied.

Coda

On Thursday the 'No Photography' sign is facing Abramović, and she is wearing a red dress. At 5.15 P.M. a young man leaves the chair, looking shattered and dazed. He is replaced by another young man. It is a late-night gallery opening, and the mood feels mean. There is applause for the young man as he leaves his seat. In the brief respite between these two men, Abramović lets her arms hang heavy by her side, the weight of her hands and arms evident in the dropping of her shoulders. In this moment, I am reminded of what she said to a much smaller crowd in The Whitworth Art Gallery, Manchester. She spoke about 'vampirism', about how sometimes the people you meet need too much from you, and they leech your energy, take too much out of you. Sometimes the demand is too much from you, it feels all-consuming. Abramović had a strategy to resist this happening. She suggested pressing your index finger and thumb of your right hand together, and then repeating the action on the left. Once you have closed this circuit, she suggested that you allow your tongue to rest against the roof of the mouth, pressing gently behind the teeth. The result is the creation of a closed circuit, a kind of 'feedback loop' which allows you to keep your energy intact. I let my gaze travel down her heavy arms, look at her gently reddening hands. They are soft; there is no circuit being formed. Perhaps he wasn't a vampire.

Tonight the guards seem more excited than usual. More agitated. The second young man holds eye contact for 22 minutes, and then he suddenly bows his head, like a full stop. The previous young man had done this same little punctuation with his head. At this I wondered if those waiting in the line had agreed to some sort of pact, either spoken or unspoken, to keep the engagement with Abramović short. Those waiting in line sway in anticipation, and I cannot decide what I want to call them. They aren't sitters; not yet. 'Queuers' doesn't seem quite right. Are they 'standers', 'waiters', 'plinthers'? Or maybe they become 'Ulays' in their urgent need to join Abramović.

A guard shouts, 'Five minutes . . . this area will be closed', and preparations begin for today's end. Davide moves in and greets the next waiting 'Ulay' at the edge of the square, I see her face fall as she understands and backs away in disappointment, suddenly embarrassed. Abramović has her head on the table, and suddenly there is applause. The atrium is emptied and guards ask the stragglers to leave. I am aware of the space as panoptic, and I look up to see the many windows on the floors above which over-look the atrium, filled with the smears of faces and hands. Marco moves to the front of the space, and as Abramović lifts her head for him, he takes her photograph. Davide steps forward, speaking into her ear, lightly touching her arm. He moves around the four corners of the space, switching off the stage spotlights one by one. She folds forward in her chair, head to knees. Whilst she is perched on the edge of the seat, Davide picks up the red cushion and replaces it with a cream one. And with the cushion under his left arm and Abramović under his right, he takes her weight and leads her away. Marco picks up his camera, his tripod, his bag, and also leaves. The space stands empty and still for a moment.

* * *

As we move away from the experiential and towards the analytical, it might be useful to reflect on what we learned from the experience of watching Abramović There was something curiously exposing in sitting opposite her – not because you could be 'seen'; after all, the anonymity of the crowd was waiting for the moment you left the chair – but exposing in the sense that this seemingly intimate one-to-one exchange exposed the broader mechanics of the process of audiencing. The inherently uneven nature of the exchange between audience and performer seemed to be underscored, reminding us as audience that although we were visible, we were never really the subject of analysis, something we will return to later in this section.

In her introductory essay to the 2010 edition of *About Performance,* an issue subtitled 'Audiencing: The Work of The Spectator in Live Performance', Laura Ginters observes that despite the fact that in 'all but the rarest cases, spectators are the largest number of contributors to the live performance event' (Ginters, 2010: 7), audiences have been largely omitted from theatrical scholarship. In terms of writing specifically aimed at addressing theatre audiences, 'spectators have historically been the least studied and the most generalised of all participants' (Ginters, 2010: 7). For many years, the most detailed overview of the terrain came in Susan Bennett's *Theatre Audiences.* At the time of Bennett's writing, theatre audiences had not been the focus of much consideration. As she observes, this is perhaps because the role of the audience was seen as a given, noting that

[t]he extensive criticism of reader-response theorists has not achieved a codification of reading practice, but it has made us more aware of the complexity of a process once considered 'natural'. (Bennett, 1990: 92)

Bennett's text offers an excellent account of the shifting roles of the audience and how they have been pressed into service as a cultural force. Although her book does an admirable job of bringing to the fore the otherwise marginalised role of the audience, it nevertheless (necessarily) positions the audience as a mass. In recent years, scholarship has shifted somewhat, doubtless due in part to the fact that '[i]n much contemporary theatre the audience becomes a self-conscious co-creator of performance' (Bennett, 1997: 21), a trend Bennett noted in the second edition of her book. Ginters offers an overview of the academics beginning to explore this terrain, and references the work of Bruce McConachie (2008), Dennis Kennedy (2009), Helena Grehan (2009), Rachel Fensham (2009), Alison Oddey (2009) and Christine White and Helen Freshwater (2009). These works on spectatorship are further supported by subsequent scholarship that has tended to offer a more focused consideration of audiences functioning within specific roles, exploring contexts in which the audience operates in some way outside of normative practices. An obvious example comes in the recent consideration of intimate and immersive practices evident in the writings of Martin Welton (2011), Maria Chatzichristodoulou and Rachel Zerihan (2012), Josephine Machon (2013), Gareth White (2013) and Leslie Hill and Helen Paris (2014).

In a variety of ways, each of these academics makes a response to Bennett's recognition of the shift towards an audience involved in co-creation, whether through considering implied participation in the generation of performance materials, which is to say focusing upon what might be termed 'postmodern' or 'post-dramatic' strategies, or through more explicit participation by discussing immersive and interactive processes. For our part, this chapter contributes to the debate primarily by focusing upon the complexity of audience encounters, and draws upon our experiences as performance practitioners, performer trainers and active audience members.

Since we began making practice together in the late 1990s, we have concerned ourselves with the assumptions made in the exchange between performer and audience. This chapter considers the potential significance offered through such exchanges as well as what is missed when they are overlooked. We hope to take up the implicit challenge laid down by Ginters when she states, '[I]t has become clear that we cannot and will not continue to ignore or deal summarily or merely speculatively with the spectator and the audience' (Ginters, 2010: 8).

Part of the issue with a sustained consideration of audiences seems to spring from some originary thinking on Western performance modes. In *The Republic*, Plato observed that

[f]ew I believe are capable of reflecting that to enter into another's feelings must have an effect on our own: the emotions of pity our sympathy has strengthened will not be easy to restrain when we are suffering ourselves. (Plato, 1930 [370 B.C.])

This starting point, the idea that an audience will be subsumed by a fiction and therefore cease to strive towards an understanding of 'truth', might thus be articulated as the part of the 'creation myth' of theatre; although other perspectives are offered, that original understanding of the audience as passive and disengaged seems to have somewhat infected many subsequent conceptualisations. This tension is explored in detail by Jacques Rancière, first in his article 'The Emancipated Spectator' and then in his book of the same name:

There is no theatre without spectatorship [. . .] but spectatorship is a bad thing. Being a spectator means looking at a spectacle. And looking is a bad thing, for two reasons. First, looking is deemed the opposite of knowing. It means standing before an appearance without knowing the conditions which produced that appearance or the reality that lies behind it. Second, looking is deemed the opposite of acting. He who looks at the spectacle remains motionless in his seat, lacking any power of intervention. (Rancière, 2007: 272)

Perhaps it is not just the creation myths of theatre that are to blame for this, but also the inherited nomenclature. The language of theatre is the language of reception. The English word 'theatre' has its roots in the Ancient Greek *theasthai* 'to behold', which in turn informs both the Greek and Latin words which describe the buildings in which performances are staged (*theatron* and *theatrum*). 'Audience' and 'auditorium' both come from the Latin *audire,* 'to hear'. These two key linguistic markers make no account of the embodied. As Ginters elegantly asks, 'Why does this "corporeal presence but [. . .] slippery concept" (Kennedy 2009, 3) have an etymology based in the visual in the singular and the auditory in the collective?' (Ginters, 2010: 8). Both words foreground reception over generation or contribution. It is particularly interesting that the language of reception (audience) itself reinforces the idea of passivity and resists the potential for action. It is, at least in part, this inaction that Rancière is offering a resistance to in his call for emancipation. The spectatorial focus from which the audience member is seeking release is situated in the landscape of the external. As Rancière observes (*pace* Feuerbach and Debord), 'The spectacle is in the realm of vision. Vision means externality. Now externality means the dispossession of one's own being. "The more man contemplates, the less he is," Debord says' (Rancière, 2007: 274). The critique goes thus: visuality equates to externality, and externality is a fleeing of the senses from the body towards an imagined or projected other, an other which, certainly in Plato's terms, offers no potential for 'truth'. Whether or not it is a concern for the lack of 'truth' remains open to debate, but it seems likely that it is this sense of inactivity and the resulting loss of agency that has led to a consideration of interactive models of performance as means of resistance.

In her consideration of Jeremy Deller's 2001 multimode art work (taking the form of re-enactment, exhibition, film and bookwork) *The Battle of Orgreave,* Claire Bishop observes that

the binary of active versus passive hovers over any discussion of participatory art and theatre, to the point where participation becomes an end in itself: as

Rancière so pithily observes, 'Even when the dramaturge or the performer does not know what he wants the spectator to do, he knows at least that the spectator has to do something: switch from passivity to activity.' (Bishop, 2012: 37)

Through her invocation of Rancière, Bishop reminds the reader that the acceptance of the binary is to end in an unproductive stalemate, a position which does little to move the debate surrounding the audience/performer dynamic forward. What is interesting for us is how Rancière goes on to complete this observation:

[W]hy not turn things around? Why not think, in this case too, that it is precisely the attempt at suppressing the distance that constitutes the distance itself? Why identify the fact of being seated motionless with inactivity, if not by the presupposition of a radical gap between activity and inactivity? Why identify 'looking' with 'passivity' if not by the presupposition that looking means looking at the image or the appearance, that it means being separated from the reality that is always behind the image? (Rancière, 2007: 26)

In this respect, he is opening up the presumed binary to critique by asking how the presumptive link between visuality and passivity might be unsettled. Certainly, there is enough theory regarding visuality as a means of active agency that might allow us to unsettle the assertion that to spectate is to absolve oneself of all action. The most obvious (and some might say insidious) would be Laura Mulvey's conceptualisation of the male gaze; a visual touchstone that, despite critique, remains an active way of understanding the potential power that looking can hold. The gaze is positioned as an action that has the potential to remove agency from the object of the gaze while reinforcing the primacy of the subjective position doing the looking. Thus, to be engaged in looking is to have power; looking has an agency all of its own. And one need not only think of the problematic position of the scopophilic as a way in which the spectator is given agency.

The idea of witness offers a certain weight of responsibility, suggesting as it does participation in an action. In a variety of legal processes, from marrying to buying a house, a witness is required to allow the exchanges to occur. Indeed, within a marriage ceremony it is those who witness the event that allow the ceremony to be successfully concluded. It is by calling upon those present to witness the ceremony that it can be recognised by law. Thus, the witness is an active participant in the event. Similarly, the term 'witness' is used in Authentic Movement, an improvisatory approach to dance which sees the practitioner finding movement from within. Started by Mary Starks Whitehouse and developed by Janet Adler, Authentic Movement sees the mover observed by a witness whose role is to contain the experience and to watch without judgement or intervention. Despite the apparent passivity, witnesses are actively engaged as they are encouraged to notice their own sensations and experiences at the same time as watching the mover. As within a legal process, the witness is positioned as integral and within a workshop these roles will be swapped. To witness is to be central to the proceedings, to be key to the functioning of the event. This imbrication of performer and spectator allows the roles to be seen as complicit in a way that reminds us that Bennett opens her study with Grotowski's question:

> Can theatre exist without an audience? At least one spectator is needed to make it a performance. (Grotowski, 1968, in Bennett, 1990: 1)

In some ways, Abramović's *The Artist Is Present* takes Grotowski's question to its most logical conclusion. To return to Rancière, this question is answered through a recognition of theatre's roots as a community-engaged practice, with a renewed focus upon the importance of the 'reform of theatre [allowing for] the restoration of its authenticity as an assembly or a ceremony of the community' (Rancière, 2007: 274). Thus, the 'emancipation' of which Rancière writes does not refer to a freeing of the spectator as might initially be assumed, but rather a yoking of the spectator to the wider community within which she sits. It is difficult to know if that is what happened as we sat before Abramović; were we contributing to this return, in which Theatre is given back to the community that hosts it, or were we contributing to a further distancing in which spectacle and visuality replaced experience?

Perhaps an invocation of Edith and Victor Turner's *communitas* might be useful at this point. Through *communitas,* what is offered is an unstructured coming together, one that foregrounds equality, and for the Turners it opens up the potential for anti-structure, a place of transgression and sharing. What this might offer over and above community, is a recognition that through anti-structure the entire community is afforded equality, which doesn't simply mean those of low status are raised up, but also those of high status are brought low. Whether this is a concept that has any long-term potential within extant communities is not for debate here; rather, it is the potential for emancipation of an audience that is being considered. In spectatorial contexts, *communitas* has the potential to open up lines of communication that might not be possible in other, more entrenched communities. Audiences are temporary, and as such there is less at stake in the renegotiation of cultural position, so any shifts in power are limited to the life of the performance. To return to Claire Bishop's discussion of *The Battle of Orgreave,* the potential for *communitas* in participatory art becomes evident:

> The reason why Deller's *The Battle of Orgreave* has become such a *locus classicus* of recent participatory art [. . .] seems to be because it is ethically commendable (the artist worked closely in collaboration with former miners) as well as irrefutably political: using a participatory performance and mass media to bring back into popular consciousness 'an unfinished messy history' of the state crushing the working class and turning it against itself. (Bishop, 2012: 35)

In many respects, Deller's *Orgreave* relies on *communitas* to come into being, and it is through a parity of experience and ownership that the materiality of the artwork functions. Bishop is not blind, however, to the potential pitfalls of taking socially engaged practice and working it through for location within a high-art context: 'Of course, at this point there is usually the objection that artists who end up exhibiting their work in galleries and museums compromise their projects' social and political aspirations' (Bishop, 2012: 37). She goes on to offer a qualification of this critique, when she suggests the following:

> The binary of active/passive is reductive and unproductive, because it serves only as an allegory of inequality. This insight can be extended to the argument that high culture, as found in art galleries, is produced for and on behalf of the ruling classes; by contrast, 'the people' (the marginalised, the excluded) can only be emancipated by direct inclusion in the production of a work. This argument – which also underlies arts funding agendas influenced by policies of social inclusion – assumes that the poor can only engage physically, while the middle classes have the leisure to think and critically reflect. (Bishop, 2012: 38)

Here, the spectatorial versus the embodied takes on another level of complexity. Embodiment is reduced to 'unthinking' or lacking critical engagement, yet another unhelpful binary that further reinforces the Cartesian error. The body becomes analogue for 'the people', and the people become material for the artist to manipulate and for the critically engaged audience to consume. In the context of Deller's *Orgreave*, this would result in an exoteric/esoteric binary aesthetic. The exoteric refers that to which the majority can relate, or understand. It references a populist tradition, as opposed to the esoteric, which suggests understanding from a limited, particular group. Broadly put, the exoteric encompasses the majority of the participants and 'live' witnesses, 'first-hand participants of the event in 2001, and those watching them from the field (primarily Yorkshire locals)' (Bishop, 2012: 37) and watching broadcast footage on UK TV station, Channel Four, whereas the esoteric speaks to the few, 'those who read the book and listen to the CD of interviews; and those who view the archive/installation in the Tate's collection' (Bishop, 2012: 37). Such binaries, although intended to offer a critique of the apparent inequality between artist and participant, and doubtless intended to problematise the 'ownership' of such materials, further reinforces sociocultural positioning, rather than allowing for *communitas* and anti-structure, with Bishop observing in the case of Orgreave that '[t]he effect of this argument is to reinstate the prejudice by which working-class activity is restricted to manual labour' (Bishop, 2012: 38).

Finding a way to resist the binary of active/passive, might be usefully explored through what has been articulated as 'the affective turn', a theorisation of complex social interaction which places emphasis on the bodily experience. Often connected to emotional states, although not positioned as synonymous with them, the field of affect studies grows out of the writings of Baruch Spinoza, specifically his *Ethics*. We will consider the landscape of affect in more detail in the next section, but thought it helpful to introduce the idea here, due to the following explanation from Brian Massumi:

> The concept of affect that I find most useful is Spinoza's well-known definition. Very simply, he says that affect is 'the capacity to affect or be affected'. This is deceptively simple. First, it is directly relational, because it places affect in the space of relation: between an affecting and a being affected. It focuses on the middle, directly on what happens between. More than that, it forbids separating passivity from activity. (Massumi, 2015: 91)

The idea is that an affective state resists the separation of action from passivity because, like *communitas*, it has an explicitly political dimension which precludes a witness from being passive because the alteration of her bodily states are informed by the very act of witnessing. Although this doesn't quite solve the politically divided viewership suggested by Bishop, it does remind us of our own complicity in the act of watching. When we (and remember that by 'we' and 'us', we are not generalising, but referring to the two authors, Bob and Lee) watch performance, we are responsible for our responses. To reflect back on the way we began this section and our experience of sitting with Abramović during *The Artist Is Present*, this seems not only fraught with ideological problems but also offers serious issues in relation to the valorisation of the singular viewpoint, an idealised perspective that was never really available. If a focus is placed upon documentary accounts, what we might term the 'politics of the body' is lost, and we miss the potentiality afforded by performance, which Rebecca Schneider suggests offers

---

Towards the climax of Punchdrunk's *The Drowned Man*, I found myself being taken by the hand, and led through the crowd in front of me. The young woman in the slip dress kept looking back at me, squeezing my hand reassuringly. We moved at quite a pace, dodging and weaving. She held me tightly, and I started to feel anxious about my palms. Were they too sweaty? Would she be grossed out? I didn't want this to be the case. After all, we had a connection, we must have. She chose me.

We manoeuvred our way through a variety of rooms, her leading, me following. We went down corridors, past slower groups, heading towards the big open space I had been dozing in an hour earlier. The crush of bodies pushed us towards one another, and her grip on my hand tightened. With her other hand she clasped my upper arm, my bicep. Still holding my arm, she let go of my hand, and snaked her arm around me, sliding her hand into my lower back. We were pushed into a sort of embrace. She turned her gaze towards me, her neck craning. Suddenly I was acutely aware of my height. At 6'2'', I felt every inch. Big, sweaty, ungainly. Held by a woman probably young enough to be my daughter. And that realisation from nowhere, making me wonder if I had been thinking of this as some kind of romantic or erotic encounter, brought me up short again. I didn't think I had been, but I realised that the script open to me was limited. The wider text of the piece was painfully heteronormative, with coupling after coupling filling the spaces. From the opening semi-orgy in the nightclub, the atmosphere had been libidinally charged. As this women held me, guided me, gazed at me, I didn't feel there was any other narrative available for me to fall into. Thankfully, just as I was beginning to feel more awkward as the sweat from my back made my T-shirt stick to me, the crowd swelled once more, and in the buffeting we were pulled apart.

a challenge to the 'ocular hegemony' that, to quote Kobena Mercer, 'assumes that the visual world can be rendered knowable before the omnipotent gaze of the eye and the 'I' of the Western cogito (1996: 165). Thus there is a political promise in this equation of performance with disappearance: if performance can be understood as disappearing, perhaps performance can rupture the ocular hegemony Mercer states. (Schneider, 2012: 64)

Although it is true that the presence we experienced in *The Artist Is Present* had one eye on the archive, with the omnipresent gaze of Marco Anelli's camera positioning each sitter as a literal photo opportunity, with each photograph offering a chance to claim 'I was there', it cannot overwrite the embodied responses of our spectatorship.

To some extent, this assumes that there is indeed something happening in the moment of exchange. Even our decision to articulate it as a 'moment of exchange' strongly indicates our bias towards the belief that the interaction is an active one. We consider those moments of obvious and explicit interaction throughout the course of this writing, but it is our belief that all performances have the capacity for some form of intersubjective exchange (a territory we explore in greater depth in the following section). In the early years of the twentieth century, Norman Triplett became interested in the effect executing a task in a group had on the successful outcome of the task. He noticed that those participating in a task together were more likely to successfully complete the task, and that the task would be completed more quickly. He referred to this as the 'social facilitation effect', an observation that would go on to have an impact upon social and sports psychology. This observation also became known as the 'audience effect' and continued to be explored throughout the twentieth century. Explorations of the audience effect led to understandings regarding the presence of an audience upon the completion of a task, and were considered as both positive and negative. These early considerations of the audience positioned it as a microcosm of society, and the presence of this group seemed to have implications for both improved response as well as social inhibition. For the purposes of this book, the success or failure and the overall impact of the audience on those executing the task is less relevant than the way in which experiments such as these have impacted upon how the audience is conceptualised. In these experiments, the audience is offered as a force, like gravity. Its presence effects the execution of a task for better or worse, and the impact upon the actant is the focus of consideration and analysis. The exchange is figured as a one-way process; the audience can affect the performer, but there is no specific attention paid to the performer's impact upon the audience. This is not offered as a critique of the experiments; rather, it is to highlight the cultural assumptions upon which such experiments draw. Triplett, and those that followed him, saw the audience as a mass, a singular unified body that, because of its collective construction, has the power to stand in for society at large.

In order to make any headway in understanding what passes between the audience and the performer, there is a need to consider the physical space between and what might happen therein. This space has traditionally been considered through proxemics, reader response or a combination of both. Although we undoubtedly need to draw upon these filters, our intention is to also consider the intersubjective as a way in which to understand the experience of spectatorship and to consider how this might inform an affective response to performance materials. In his book *Performance*, Julian Hilton turned to the work of 1960s anthropologist Edward T. Hall as a means to understand the geographies and architectures of performance. Hilton foregrounds the importance of a proxemic engagement as a means to unpack the interpersonal exchange within performer/audience dynamics and how distance and proximity might impact upon potential readings. According to Edward T. Hall:

> The proxemic relations between people [divide] into four main categories: intimate, personal, social and public. The exact dimensions of these zones is variable according to culture. (1987: 22)

Hilton's overview takes Hall's socially grounded concepts and applies these ideas to the field of performance practice. There is clear and immediate value in this approach. By taking the four striations offered by Hall, Hilton is able to begin to encourage the reader to think about her experience as a spectator. By offering some clear examples, he discusses the audience's relative distance from the stage and considers this through the lens of Hall's proxemics. This approach is developed by Leslie Hill and Helen Paris in their book *Performing Proximity*. Like Hilton, they use Hall's conceptualisation of proxemics as a means to address what happens in the moment of a performative exchange. As performance makers and academics (they assert that '[w]e are artists first and scholars second in terms of chronology – the order in which we approach ideas [Hill and Paris, 2013: 3]), their writing focuses upon the specifics of their own performance making and as such is more interested in the intimate layer of Hall's taxonomy. In an attempt to understand the significance of proximity in general, they quote Hall as a means to consider how the space in between individuals impacts upon selfhood:

> Man's sense of space is closely related to his sense of self, which is in an intimate transaction with his environment. Man can be viewed as having visual, kinaesthetic, tactile, and thermal aspects of his self which may be either inhibited or encouraged to develop by his environment. (Hall in Hill and Paris, 2014: 6)

For Hilton, and Hill and Paris, the proxemics of Hall are a significant way to understand the literal space in between the spectator and the performer and to consider how this might inform the figurative space and thus the subsequent opportunities for exchange. For Hill and Paris, the exploration of Hall's taxonomy of proxemics functions as a means to drill down into the specifics of their own performance-making experience. In their introduction Hill and Paris state that

> [w]riting this book is our way of synthesizing and sharing our experiences of performing to audiences in close physical proximity, sometimes close enough to reach out and touch each other, sometimes close enough to see the patterns in each other's irises. (Hill and Paris, 2014: 1)

This affecting image makes very clear the intimacies specific to the work of Hill and Paris – who perform under the company name Curious. They write from the position of the performance maker, and they look out towards the audience, even if the distance of the gaze extends only a few inches. Indeed, they are very clear that this is the focus and the direction of their concern:

> This book is performer-oriented in its approach to ideas and experiences. It's about the impact of space and proximity in relation to actual

performances rather than abstract or virtual notions of proximity and spectatorship. It deals with specific performers, specific performances and sometimes specific audience members. (Hill and Paris, 2014: 2)

The intimacy they explore is grounded in their experiences and informed by an understanding of Hall's intimate space; the understanding of intimacy offered is one which is predicated upon close physical proximity. Their practice is offered in contrast to more normative patterns of performance exchange. They offer a distinction between their work and work presented in a mid-sized theatre where 'an audience member would be very hard-pressed to get a seat within 25 feet of the actors' (Hill and Paris, 2014: 8) – a distance defined by Hall as 'public-far'. Hill and Paris offer a detailed account of the varying sizes and concomitant experiential gaps that might open up in a range of London theatre venues through the application of Edward T. Hall's 'proxemic zones'. In the context of traditional performance practice, intimacy becomes more difficult to achieve, or at least it does if we are to align intimacy with proximity.

Evidently, Hall's approach to the proxemics of personal and social space is an invaluable way to think through the concept of intimacy; however, intimacy is only one way to think about the potential for affective shifts in audience/performer interaction. As Hall suggests, the human experience is one of complexity, drawing upon a range of embodied processes which in turn impact the cognitive and emotional aspects of the self. Relative proximity or distance evidently have the potential to impact upon experience and are part of the narrative of the intersubjective exchange. That said, there are other factors that mitigate against the exclusivity of proxemics. The para-social[1] allows for a deep sense of connection to develop between the performer and the spectator, a connection that might occur despite both temporal and geographic distance. This exchange can feel intimate for the spectator, even if the performer is unaware of her presence. As outlined in Bob's experience of *The Artist Is Present*, intimacy is not guaranteed by proximity, any more than it is denied by distance. Similarly, an exchange that might be typified as intimate when measured against the understanding of proxemics may well meet the requirements in terms of

---

[1] See the section on Qualia for a discussion of the para-social.

relative distance but offer little in the way of an affective moment. The intersubjective exchange is complex. This complexity is added to by the recognition that audiences have the potential to occupy different roles depending upon the material being engaged with.

When considering striations of audience interaction, Richard Schechner suggests that there are two distinct modes of audience engagement: the accidental audience and the integral audience (see 1994: 193–6). For Schechner, the integral audience tends to bring with it a certain amount of prior knowledge and is in some way part of the event. In a ritual context, this can impact upon the level of responsibility or the particular role that might be played by the integral spectator. In contrast is the accidental spectator, someone who is positioned more as a consumer of a cultural product. In mainstream theatre practice, the accidental audience is there for the experience, often following the 'big ticket' experience, rather than engaging in cultural exchange. Arguably, the accidental spectator is conforming to the two-step/multistep flow model, in which audiences are informed by opinion leaders (critics, etc.) and follow accordingly, responding to the material not because they are invested, but because it has been designated as a valued cultural product. Of course, any such binary model is inherently problematic as it suggests there is no place for slippage, resistance or retraining oneself in alternative modes of spectatorship. Often, as a spectator, we can hold varying degrees of 'expertness' in performance and experience of performance, oscillating through a range of positions in any given experience. Questions of expertness might perhaps begin to unpack the territory of exchange; being 'in the know' can impact significantly on our experience and the potential intersubjective exchanges that result.

In his 1987 essay 'Dramaturgy of the Spectator', Marco De Marinis considers shifts in spectatorship through the application of the term 'dramaturgy'. This is typified by a move towards a more engaged audience, one that has more investment in the generation of the performance texts being encountered. De Marinis suggests 'that we can speak of this dramaturgy of the spectator in two ways, both of which are already grammatically present in the double meaning (objective and subjective) of the possessive "of"' (De Marinis, 1987: 100). This twofold approach positions the spectator as a central part of the dramaturgical approach (akin to text or scenography) and also as a co-actant in the generation of the text. The dramaturgy of the spectator both *implicates* the audience and *belongs* to the audience, allowing it to function as a creator of the text and an element within it. Central to De Marinis's conceptualisation is the shift towards an active participation on the part of the spectator, something close to the reader Roland Barthes imagines in *S/Z* (1970). Drawing upon the writings of Umberto Eco, the concept offered by De Marinis positions his model spectator as implicated in the generation of meaning:

> Naturally, in order to speak of an active dramaturgy of the spectator, we must see her/his understanding of the performance not as some mechanical operation which has been strictly predetermined – by the performance and its producers – but rather as a task which the spectator carries out in conditions of relative independence, or, as Franco Ruffini has recently suggested, in conditions of 'controlled creative autonomy'. (1987: 101)

This idea of 'relative independence' begins to frame the dramaturgy of the spectator as a means to empower the spectator, and thus shares territory with Schechner's integral aesthetic. Unlike Schechner, De Marinis offers a critical oversight of a text which requires the spectator to complete it. His concern is that a text which is too open can only be read by those with an expert perspective, which in turn limits the potential scope of its readership. Thus, the opening up of texts can result in a closing down of potential audiences. For De Marinis, this is a pay-off required to allow for a more empowered or emancipated spectator. It is these experiences to which De Marinis refers when he observes that

> [t]he other side to the theatrical relationship, contemporaneous with the first, consists of an active cooperation by the spectator. More than just a metaphorical coproducer of the performance, the spectator is a relatively autonomous 'maker of meanings' for the performance; its cognitive and emotive effects can only be truly actualized by the audience. (De Marinis, 1987: 102)

Words such as 'co-creator' abound when discussing an audience's relationship to open texts. These shifts in understanding how an audience responds to the material presented to them or, perhaps more accurately, how an audience activates such texts inevitably lead to questions of democratisation and empowerment. As immersive and interactive performance practices become more familiar to mainstream audiences, what an audience is or perhaps does, increasingly interests academics and cultural commentators alike. Helen Freshwater's overview of audiences helpfully considers such terrain in her discussion of interactivity and the move towards immersion. However, the idea that to be more involved is to have more control, or that the invitation to engage is tantamount to a democratic space, is to somewhat misunderstand the complex and shifting power dynamic in performance practice. As Roberta Mock suggests in her essay 'Experiencing Michael Mayhew's *Away in a Manger:* Spectatorial Immersion in Durational Performance', audiences do not necessarily come equipped to encounter performance practice, and they might need to prepare: '[t]o use Jacques Rancière's terminology, a spectator has to be taught (or else teach herself) how to be emancipated, to be free to find the ways inside a performance that an artist has left open' (Mock, forthcoming). Whether the experience is didactic or auto-didactic, the implication here is that the audience does not necessarily meet the work in a state of readiness, but instead a certain amount of preparation is required. Our own experience of spectatorship has led us to consider this idea of preparation, and we have written about the potential for spectatorial training strategies[2], a process which appears to reinforce the idea that the disparity between audience and performer necessitates a commitment from the spectator to find strategies to meet the work.

What is less clear is whether these processes of training, which can be positioned as a surrender of sorts, are actually empowering or democratising. They may well be instructive; they may result in a richer experience; but there is not any assurance that this is somehow an equal exchange. Freshwater begins her consideration of interaction by discussing 'the now infamous *Rhythm 0*' (Freshwater, 2009: 62) and reflects RoseLee Goldberg's account and Peggy Phelan's discussion of the audience as co-creators. Without wishing to seem dismissive of the generosity of exchange offered by Phelan, we feel that there remain significant questions around the principle of licence. Co-creation may well sound like an opportunity for equality, but there is not a concomitant sharing of prestige or profit, or indeed any sharing of the burden of loss – fiscal or reputational – that might emerge. The rhetoric of the co-creator, although

---

[2] See Whalley and Miller (2013) 'Look Right Through', in *Theatre, Dance and Performance Training*, 4:1, 102–12.

appearing to empower the audience, does so only within the limited scope of what is allowed. Even within a score as open as *Rhythm 0,* in which Abramović provided a series of objects from which her spectators could choose, it was always within Abramović's gift to allow her audience the room to define the process of engagement. Similarly, it was her power to cede that ultimately saw a loaded gun pointed at her. To be clear, this is not a claim that Abramović abnegated responsibility, any more than we accept the rhetoric that she 'asked for it'. Rather, the conditions she created allowed space for the experience to devolve into what is now remembered as a notorious *Lord of The Flies* moment or, to take a more positive view, an example of Rancière's politics and dissensus in action. What remains in question is whether the spectator is transformed through this moment of emancipation or whether the specific exchanges are contingent, tied to the room or the location in which they are enacted. If this is the case, and the emancipatory exchange is not portable to another experience, then claims for the democratisation of performance practice are open to critique. As a result, we would suggest that Freshwater's decision to employ the term 'empowerment' offers more scope in debating the shifts that might arise in interactive and immersive models of performance practice.

To return to where we opened this section, were we 'empowered' by our engagement with *The Artist Is Present?* It's difficult to say. Clearly Bob felt a responsibility to stay, to engage until the point at which the work became meaningful to her in some way. Is this empowerment or merely the product of the weight of cultural expectation? Did we feel responsible to the piece to complete it, responsible to Abramović to connect with her, or responsible to those audience members behind us in the queue? Or perhaps the responsibility is to our role as 'expert witness', as academics being supported in our viewing of the work. Judging by the number of question marks in the previous sentences, it is clear that a level of uncertainty surrounds the experience.

There are further tensions around empowerment, given that the exchanges entered into are heavily monitored. We have already written about the multiple possible audiences, viewing both Abramović and the sitters. At the risk of hyperbole, there was a sense of Jeremy Bentham's panopticon at play, an inescapable observation throughout the process of queuing. The multiple vantage points, the people waiting in the queue behind, the omnipresent webstream,

the windows from other floors overlooking the atrium – all contrib-
uted to the weight of the gaze(s). This sense of monitoring extended
to the manner in which the guards 'policed' the environment.
Any transgressions (and there were many) were shut down. The
accepted behaviours of those sitting opposite were limited and in
many regards scripted. The guards' behaviours ossified around the
performance, repositioning what was framed as a malleable interaction to a fixed, sculptural object.

Although Bennett, De Marinis and Schechner offer us ways to
interrogate the role, function and ideological conditions of the
audience, and immersive and interactive practices appear to offer
resistant strategies, as we have suggested above, there remains an
habituated tendency to consider the audience as a passive mass to be
manipulated, as is evidenced by the MoMA guards' scripted behaviours. Writing in the UK newspaper *The Guardian,* James McQuaid
(National Trust, Visitor Experience Consultant) reflects upon the
2014 Arts Marketing Association conference. In his article he references the suggestion made by National Arts Strategies President
Russell Willis Taylor that 'we need to position audiences within our
organisations as partners and consider very carefully the nature of
our relationship with them' (McQuaid, 2014: unpaginated). At face
value this may well seem like a move on the part of arts organisations to find more and clearer strategies for audience engagement
and to move towards a more integrated, even interactive, role for
audiences. However, the move to position audiences as partners
seems to be informed by the anxiety around arts organisations los-
ing cultural relevance. Implicit within this is the sense that is within
the gift of arts organisations to invite the audience in. It presupposes
a them/us binary in which the power is held on one side. McQuaid's
argument is for the continued relevance of arts organisations in
a context of twenty-four-hour news cycles, narrowcasting and the
'YouTube generation'. McQuaid's anxiety is that the technological
shift which allows for a context of user-generated material muddies
the distinctions between high, popular and amateur cultural product. In the landscape of user-generated culture (what we might have
once deemed 'amateur'), the accidental/integral binary is unsettled.
The shift away from the two-step/multistep flow model removes
the need for opinion leaders (in this instance curators, funders, etc.),
allowing audiences autonomy and the space to create the product
they feel is missing. With popularity of material easily monetised

through pre-existing models, the them/us, or even the accidental/ integral aesthetic, are eroded. YouTube has proven how users can monetise their video output, and crowd sourcing is fast becoming a way for artists to remove the need to engage with Arts Council England funding processes and the structures they impose. Whether this is a move towards a democratisation or merely a different stage in the commodification of arts practice remains to be seen.

Although the debate is an interesting one, it is important that we do not become sidetracked here into a conversation around 'worth' or 'value'. These debates are less interesting to us than what the interrogation of a them/us binary means for the spectator. Despite the theoretical claims made by Bennett, De Marinis, Schechner and others, McQuaid's position would seem to suggest that the audience as passive mass remains the default perspective in current cultural dialogue. The 'value' or 'worth' of user-generated content is less interesting than the implication for a reassessing of the performer/ audience dynamic. What is at stake in the shift that McQuaid is addressing is the potential for a different understanding of this dynamic. When the cultural capital of Bourdieu is challenged, then the potential for intersubjective exchange shifts dramatically. It would seem that in the attempt to make a case for the continued importance of arts organisations as a primary mode of engagement with cultural practices, McQuaid potentially overwrites the value of cultural pluralism and the multivocality that user-generated con-tent affords. To be clear, McQuaid's concerns are not driven by self-interest, but from a real concern over the potential implications for devolving all decisions regarding cultural activities to market forces. The unintentional binary offered by McQuaid reminds us of Bennett's reference to Jill Dolan's writing and her recognition of the cultural exclusivity of much theatrical practice with the assertion that 'mainstream theatre addresses an audience which is white, male, middle class, and heterosexual' (Bennett, 1990: 95), which in turn can be seen to support the integral/accidental behav-iours addressed by Schechner. Each in its way seems to accept that there is (or, for McQuaid, should be) a certain level of exclusivity to the process of being an audience member. We are aware that McQuaid's commentary is specific to a UK context, given that it relies on a subsidised system funded by central government. Of course, McQuaid's concern offers a broader cause for concern too, in that it envisions a shift towards a populist landscape that will be valued by the number of clicks, likes or re-tweets, which might call into question the potential for diversity, quite apart from what the implications might be for quality.

We opened this section by thinking about how a them/us binary in audience/performer studies might be resisted. This soon developed into a resistance of further split within the conceptualising of an audience as active or passive. As we draw this section to a close, how then might we resist the tendency towards all binaries in discussions of audience behaviour, and the attendant implication of hierarchical exchange? One potential strategy is to consider how shifts in the scholarship around performance have interrogated what performance is, and the concomitant recognition of a multiplicity of audience behaviours. There are many potential routes into this debate, but perhaps the most inclusive is through the work of Jon McKenzie. In his book *Perform or Else,* McKenzie avoids binary oppositions (that which is performance and that which is not) by offering three paradigms that form a large 'performance' site. The discipline and practice of performance is described by three models: organisational performance, cultural performance and technical performance. Organisational performance is defined by McKenzie through an analysis of the front cover of *Forbes* magazine (a business publication), and it is from this publication that McKenzie takes the title of his book: *Perform or Else.* This form of performance describes workplace activities which fit into the corporate structure. Whether looking at huge conglomerates or non-profit-making organisations, McKenzie defines a mode of performance management that is driven by efficiency and efficacy. Cultural performance is broadly defined as an area mapped out by Carlson, Goldberg, Schechner and other scholars working in the field of performance studies. The final area of technological performance is articulated through the application of science models and describes the functions of technical systems such as engineering or computer science. By offering this expanded consideration of performance, McKenzie opens up the term to include a range of disparate practices, and in so doing implicitly questions the role of an audience. His thesis echoes and builds upon Elin Diamond's observation that 'performance is always a doing and a thing done' (Diamond, 1996: 1). These multimodal understandings of performance can have significant implications for the audience, removing as it does the clean distinction between roles. Even without McKenzie's expanded model, shifts in the understanding of what he refers to as cultural performance, have changed significantly the position of the audience. Scholarship in the broad field of performance studies has marked a significant shift in the cultural value of knowledge and in an increased recognition of interdisciplinary and multidisciplinary practices. As Diana Taylor has observed:

> Western culture, wedded to the word, whether written or spoken, enables language to usurp epistemic and explanatory power. Performance studies allows us to take seriously other forms of cultural expression as both praxis and episteme. Performance traditions also serve to store and transmit knowledge. Performance studies, additionally, functions as a wedge in the institutional understanding and organization of knowledge. (Taylor, in Schechner, 2002: 7)

This transmission of knowledge through more embodied modes has a direct impact on the role and importance of any audience. If, as is suggested by Taylor, the performance traditions might 'serve to store and transmit knowledge', the importance of reception shifts. A performance cannot transmit knowledge without an audience to witness it. Of course, the same might be said of written discursive strategies; the knowledge generated by this book is of questionable value if no one reads it. However, it is the means of reception that is open to debate. The reading of a book or article is primarily a solo activity; even if it is supported by reading groups and seminars, the initial work is done alone. Contrast this with the transmission of knowledge in performance, which for the most part is engaged with as a group. Even in one-to-one performance practice, there are two subject positions in the space at any given time. If we return to *The Artist Is Present,* the experience is shared and witnessed, even in the moment when the spectator sits opposite Abramović. Couple this with the recognition that the everyday can be positioned as a performance (a concept which found articulation in the theoretical writings of Erving Goffman as well as the dramatic performances of Allan Kaprow), and the exploration of cultural performance shifts significantly the understanding of the term 'audience'.

In his exploration of the debate, Schechner suggests that performance studies utilises two modes of observation: the mode which allows some activities to function in the position of 'is performance' while allowing the mode in which other activities are positioned 'as performance', as 'there are limits to what "is" performance. But just about anything can be studied "as" performance. Something "is" a performance when historical and social context, convention, usage and tradition say it is' (Schechner, 2002: 30). This distinction is useful for understanding the importance of the audience in taking ownership of their own experience. Although it takes cultural consensus to position something definitively as a performance (the 'is performance' category), anything that catches the eye of a spectator can be positioned, and subsequently read, 'as performance'. In the terrain of performance art, these distinctions are in flux; contemporary news footage of *The Artist Is Present* positioned the work as a 'staring contest', but its location within the Marron Atrium of MoMA suggests a certain level of cultural consensus having been achieved. Since performance studies has developed as a discipline (and as a result informed the focus of such related fields as drama and theatre studies), its consideration of some activities 'as' performance has allowed these events to benefit from a shift in the cultural consensus, which has resulted in them becoming read as 'is' performance. As the 'canon' of performance art has grown, so too has an understanding of audience behaviours. This development of 'canonical' performance art texts is exacerbated by the suggestion that '[t]he relationship between studying performance and doing performance is integral' (Schechner, 2002: 1), and this relationship sees many practitioners contributing to the academic writing informing both areas. As a result, the 'as'/'is' binary becomes more difficult to distinguish, further contributing to the complexities of the term 'performance' and the implications for the term 'audience'.

It seems necessary that conversations continue around what is meant by the term 'audience' but also what is expected of their behaviours. Although the engagement of audiences of immersive theatre such as Punchdrunk's *The Drowned Man* and the interactive practices of performance art have begun to inform these debates, questions around the extent to which autonomy and co-creation are possible remain live. It is also necessary to foreground the potential ideological issues which stem from these developments. Evidently, performance art has found vocal support in the university sector, with many of the leading practitioners doing double duty as academics, teaching in undergraduate and postgraduate programmes. For example, between 1973 and 1997, Abramović taught at the Academy of Arts, Novi Sad, Serbia; the Académie des

Beaux-Arts, Paris, France; the Hochschule der Künste, Berlin, Germany; and the Hochschule für Bildende Künste, Hamburg. She also holds honorary doctorates of the arts from both Plymouth University, United Kingdom (2009) and Instituto Superior de Arte, Cuba (2012) in recognition of her artistic and pedagogic practice.

It could be argued that much of the discourse around the development of audience interaction has been an esoteric debate which bears little relation to the engagement of the majority of audiences, a critique that we are well aware could similarly be levelled at this writing, coming as it does from two theatre academics working in higher education. Although Bennett wrote that '[t]heatre no longer remains the sole domain of the educated and economically-able few [. . .] democratisation is not only seen as desirable, but as a crucial aspect of new developments in performance and theory' (Bennett, 1990: 10–11), the observation is nearly thirty years old, and one arguably not borne out in contemporary British contexts. The savage cuts to UK arts funding in 2011 continue to have implications as to who has access to theatrical product, not least because of the unequal distribution of Arts Council England (ACE) funding. Predicted ACE spend for 2015–18 suggests that £689m (43.4%) will be invested in the arts in London, with £900m to be invested in the rest of England. This would mean a per capita return of £81.87 per head of population (php) in London, with the rest of England receiving a per capita return of £19.80 php. Or if you prefer, a spend in favour of London of 4.1:1. The overall landscape of public funding for arts in the United Kingdom is encapsulated by Christopher Gordon, David Powell and Peter Stark thusly:

> The Hard Facts report illustrates the absence of any strategic support of participation in the arts at local level and the proven contribution that such work can make to individual and community wellbeing. The longer term research framework of the report also reveals what appears to be an undeclared policy to shed smaller companies from the ACE's national portfolio (a net loss of 352 since 2007/8), a continuing failure to address cultural diversity in the country and worrying inconsistencies in the operation of grant programmes. (Gordon, Powell and Stark, 2014)

As with the earlier questions of 'value' of 'worth' that emerged from a consideration of McQuaid, cultural capital and exclusionary social policies are not the primary focus of this section, but nor can we be blind to the debate. As academics working in higher education in the United Kingdom, questions of accessibility (both fiscal and physical) are central to much of the teaching we are engaged in. We recognise that the ideological implications of exclusion speak (in the UK at least) to class positioning, ethnic background and regionality. All are of great import and worthy of detailed consideration and continued analysis. That being said, this book is not the place to offer a full-throated discussion of these concerns. Instead, we have ascribed to the idea that the personal is political, and hope that through the decision to foreground the experiential as a way in to debating the intersubjective exchange between audience and performer, we (and this includes you as reader) might be able to use our own experiences, our own cultural position and our own bodies as a strategies of resistance. These bodies we occupy will necessarily reveal themselves through the writing, perhaps allowing us to return to and unpick significant moments of cultural tension.

It is pertinent here to remind ourselves what we believe this writing is doing. Ultimately, we believe that we are writing about our particular take on how to be an audience. If this is indeed the case, it is important that we don't appear to be offering a 'how-to' guide. We are not offering you some definitive way to train yourself to be an audience member, in part because it would be a somewhat redundant task; the only real way to train as an audience is to go and watch things. Decide what you like and what you don't, and keep challenging your own expectations and prejudices. This is probably the closest we will come to giving you advice as to how you might become a 'better' member of the audience. Instead of advice, we want to offer you actions, tasks that will hopefully take you into a more mindful engagement with the process of watching.

As we move towards these tasks, we would like to consider some of the things we think have happened in the exchange. Although Bennett offers the term 'democratisation' to describe the shift in audience roles, we remain uncertain if this is something which can be achieved, or even if the aim is a valuable one. Certainly there have been attempts to offer resistant tropes for what is seemingly considered an established and understood engagement (Boal's 'spectactor' (1973/2008) comes to mind), and even with early attempts from practitioners such Marinetti, whose attempt to shift away from the passivity of fourth-wall naturalism towards a more evenly distributed process of engagement does so through the device of the audience having something done to them. The use of itching or sneezing powder, glue on the seats or the deliberate double selling of seating (see Bennett, 1990: 5), at a fundamental level differs little from Meyerhold's flanking of the proscenium arch with large mirrors in an attempt to break down the fissure between the audience and the stage. Throughout these attempts the audience is merely reminded of its position as the passive mass who has these actions acted upon its members.

Thus, the position, and the role of the audience opens itself up as a site of contested ideological debate. Although there are doubtless significant shifts emerging out of higher education and scholarship, these might potentially exclude wider audiences, not by design, but by access. Similarly, the opening up of multiplatform creativity, with smartphones, tablets and laptop computers (a collection of words guaranteed to date this argument much more than its year of publication) containing apps and software which significantly aid and potentially 'democratise' the creation and sharing of user-generated content. At the same time this apparent democratisation might only be a further capitulation to a market economy where clicks replace cash. Interactivity and immersion allow for more active involvement, leading to the language of co-creation, but always within a predetermined set of appropriate responses. In all these instances, and more besides, we seem to be surfacing the recognition that to be an audience continues to be a political act, one freighted with significant social and ideological implications.

Ultimately, the idea of co-creation or the use of the term 'democratisation' opens as many areas of concern as it resolves. The idea that the audience are offered more autonomy as they step out of the mass and into the singular appears to make sense, at least in principle. However, it is helpful to reflect upon the extent to which this singularity requires a sense of policing. To return one last time to *The Artist Is Present,* the resistant strategies employed by spectators are the exception which proves the rule. On the final day of the installation, we witnessed three such interruptive engagements, each closed down rather than being subsumed into the larger project. During the last sitting, one woman who had been waiting in the line approached Abramović while pulling her dress off over her head. As she walked towards her, naked, this interloper was approached by multiple guards and removed from the space. We choose our words

carefully here because the engagements are already 'high tempera-
ture' without us offering descriptions such as 'tackled by the guards'
or 'forcibly removed', but these might be closer to our memory of
the event. Certainly, we wondered what was so transgressive about
this woman's flesh, when there were multiple interactions of previous work by Abramović being re-enacted on the sixth floor. In this
room – no less accessible, no less busy – multiple nudes, male and
female, re-performed work from Abramović's back catalogue. The
interruptive quality of this would-be sitter was thus lost, not just on
the two of us, but on many of those whom we heard talking about
the event in the atrium. Her attempt at meeting Abramović on her
own terms was made more visible, more transgressive by the manner in which it was censored.

A less confrontational, but no less successful incursion came in
the form of a simple leaflet drop from one of the bridges that overlooked the atrium. These leaflets, taking the form of much propa-
gandist material, laid out a resistant manifesto of anti-art. As with
the woman who stripped her dress off, the leaflets were quickly
removed, with guards asking those who had caught them mid-flut-
ter to hand them over. It was interesting to observe a certain level of
compliance, with many people dutifully passing them to the guards.

Of a somewhat different order was the projectile vomiter. This
was an attempt made by a member of the crowd to vomit at or on
Abramović. Despite being in the atrium at the time of this incursion, neither of us saw the moment itself. We have no sense of who
made the attempt, if it was a man or a woman, only that it was
deliberate, and that the clean-up was swift. Understanding why this
might be deemed transgressive is easier, but the action itself hardly
lies out with the broader actions of performance art. Vomit has
appeared in the work of Viennese Actionist Otmar Bauer, whose
1968 piece *Zeigt,* which saw him dressed in a suit while vomiting
onto a dining table, through to performance artist Millie Brown,
famed for vomiting on Lady Gaga's breasts in the performance of
their piece *Swine* at the 2014 South by South West (SXSW) Music
Festival. While offering a certain level of cultural resistance, these
are practices that are, if not exactly mainstream, certainly recognisable. The policing of the event is brought into stark contrast when
one considers the back catalogue of Abramović playing itself out in
the same gallery as part of the larger project of *The Artist Is Present.* These strategies or, more importantly, the atrium's inability to

absorb them, allow us to ask questions about exchange, interaction and autonomy, and encourage us to reflect upon the apparent co-creative role of the audience member. True, the audience is required to activate the work, but is activation an activity of the same order of creation, and can activation allow for an autonomous engagement to be played out?

The sense that there is of a set of expected behaviours also emerges when considering the 'special' audience: those attendees who sat before Abramović multiple times. The idea of being somehow pulled out of the larger populace of sitters (themselves already made 'special' by the limited gallery attendees that made up their number, and the inclusion of their images in subsequent publications) and offered a unique status ties into the myth-making narratives central to larger aims of *The Artist Is Present* and to Abramović's planned institute in upstate New York. This 'specialness' raises questions about what impact their presence might have upon the wider viewership. The repeated presence of Paco Blancas sitting opposite Abramović twenty-one times unwittingly reinforces the 'correct' mode of engagement. If you look through the twenty-one photographs of his interactions, you will see that he is often in tears. His crying does more than merely normalise the emotional response of other sitters; it almost demands it. He becomes audience to the power audience, or 'audience (n)', and his repeated presence contributes to the policing of the appropriate script to obey in all exchanges with Abramović. His tears serve in the ossification of the overall 'eventness'; his tears function as cement. We negotiate the work through the fixity of his tears.

The position of 'audience (n)' differs from the 'ur-body', an idea which we offered as 'an impossible body, an originary referent from which we might all attempt to draw an understanding, yet still being offered in the knowledge that it does not, it cannot, exist' (Whalley and Miller, 2013: 103). We formulated the 'ur-body' as a means to consider the training potential for the audience, positioning it as a fiction from which we might begin to imagine how an audience might be 'trained' to watch. However, Blancas's body is anything but a fiction; it is a real presence that repeats itself, and with each iteration comes into being with more clarity, more certainty. His is the border from which our presencing begins.

Of course, this reading runs the risk of diminishing the very real affective and emotional responses of those sitting opposite Abramović. This is not our intention. The felt sense of the participants are theirs and theirs alone to navigate. Our position is that the script of the encounter is prescribed through the behaviours of the space, the guards in the space, the other users of the space and the tacit instruction offered by Abramović. We hope to qualify the oversimplification of the exchange that emerges when co-creation is offered as a means to explicate the transaction between the audience and the performer.

The uncanny valley, identified and used by robotics and CGI, illustrates how the human-animal representation of reality is transferred to non-human subjects who resemble human aesthetics. The uncanny valley describes a graph, created by Masahiro Mori, which is valley-shaped and where the dip refers to the comfort of the human animal compared to the human-like qualities of entities. The 'uncanny' section of the valley at the lowest point of the arc signifies the strength of a negative emotional reaction to an 'almost but not quite' human representation, which results in an abject response, and as Timothy Morton states, 'In the uncanny valley, beings are strangely familiar and familiarly strange' (Morton, 2013: 130). The zombie is a prime example of a subject with human-like qualities which is nonetheless rejected forcibly in its 'almost but not quite' presence.

My emotional response to Abramović dips into uncanny valley territory, in reading the tears shed by Abramović as not for me. She becomes my crying zombie, where I assume the ersatz nature of her emotional connection to me throughout our silent 'conversation'. The fluctuations of strangely familiar/familiarly strange thrum through our brief encounter, bringing a sense of confusion which leads to my decision to wait until I feel the encounter feels 'genuine'.

Tasks: Audience

Dear Audience,

We want to write for the audiences of performances that haven't happened yet. First off, we plan to create manifestos inspired by a performance-past that has impressed, scared, inspired, confounded and delighted us.

I, ...

agree to try my best to get lost, tired, frustrated, confused and angry, and I will only watch work that means something to me.

Signed,

....

A Manifesto of Sorts for Audiences Experiencing Any and Every Kind of Performance

We are going to start with a performance that has already been done, and been gone:

Statement. September 26, 1981
I, Tehching Hsieh, plan to do a one year performance piece.
I shall stay OUTDOORS for one year, never go inside.
I shall not go in to a building, subway, car, train, car, airplane, ship, cave, tent.
I shall have a sleeping bag.
The performance shall begin on September 26, 1981 at 2 P.M. and continue until September 26, 1982 at 2 P.M.

[signed] Tehching Hsieh
Tehching Hsieh

Now to all the performances to come:

....

Things are going to be challenging, things are going to be hard. We are going to spend some of the time moving. We will walk, we will talk, we will run (maybe). We will push ourselves and we will take our minds to strange places. We will be supportive of each other, but this will not dull a sense of criticality. We will try everything once. We will try our best not to fear the consequences. We will not get embarrassed, or if we do, we will simply push through it. We won't go out of our way to piss anybody off, and if we do we'll say sorry, but we won't second-guess ourselves and we'll always try things out. We will risk assess everything, but we won't let bureaucracy stop us from doing things. We will be the thorn in the side, or the sand in the oyster. We will create with abandon and select with care. Whenever we're uncertain, we'll ask ourselves 'WWTD?' or 'What would Tehching do?' There are probably some other things, but they will no doubt become obvious later. We can always add more as we go along.

Finally, you have to hold up your end of the bargain. So, we would like you to sign the following declaration:

Tasks: Audience

Let's start with something very simple, something portable.
This is the kind of thing that you could practice in pretty much any town or city that you happen to travel to.

Find yourself a busker.*

Stand in front of her and listen to an entire song, from beginning to end.

We would like you to pay rapt attention; think about the song choice, the lyrics, the phrasing.

It's important that you don't approach this ironically. True, you don't have to like the genre of music, but you do need to admire the skill. Our intention is not for you to mock, or to pose. It is to engage with someone performing in public, and to freely give your attention and your time.

At the end of the song, look them in the eye, applaud, say thank you, and mean it.

Money does not have to change hands. This is not about commerce, this is about generosity.

*If there isn't a busker, you can find any other type of street performer.

Tasks: Audience

Automatic Writing

1. Find a quiet spot without distractions.
2. Sit at a table or desk where you'll be comfortable, with plenty of paper and pen (or pencil).
3. Take a few moments to clear your mind.
4. Touch the pen or pencil to the paper and write continually, and do not remove pen or pencil at anytime during process.
5. Try not to consciously write anything, but just let ideas, words and phrases come out of you onto the page.
6. You may find you get stuck so just repeat words or letters or phrases until you reconnect with a flow of words.
7. You can then edit this writing for performance text or give it to someone else to edit.

Tasks: Audience

Dear Audience,
Deep mapping is a
way of reaching a
hand from the pre-
sent back as far as
can be thought/felt/
seen, and holding all
this where you stand.

Deep maps

Context
This task serves as an extension of Clifford Geertz's
anthropological theory of 'thick description', where
you dig beyond the bare bones of a narrative (thin
description) to describe the action/event in front of
you in microscopic detail.

'Deep mapping' is a concept developed by Michael
Shanks and Mike Pearson in 1994 (after William Least
Heat-Moon).

'Reflecting eighteenth century antiquarian approaches
to place, which included history, folklore, natural history and hearsay, the deep map attempts to record
and represent the grain and patina of place through
juxtapositions and interpenetrations of the historical
and the contemporary, the political and the poetic,
the discursive and the sensual; the conflation of oral
testimony, anthology, memoir, biography, natural history and everything you might ever want to say about
a place. (Mike Pearson and Michael Shanks (2001),
Theatre/Archaeology, pp. 64–65).

Tasks: Audience

Task instructions

Map through performance everything that you have experienced so far as an audience. Start outside of your chosen venue, studio/home/ shopping centre.
Enter, perform and also plan and execute a leaving.

Do a 10-minute performance.
Do a 4.5-minute performance.
Do a 1-minute performance.

Think about each mapping after you have done it, and re-evaluate before performing the next.

Tasks: Audience

Today you are going to be structuring

What is the purpose of structure?
Is it a creative space?
Is it a container?
What is contained and what is released?
How do you resist what you know?
What is an opening (and how many can you imagine)?
What does an ending look like?

Dear Audience,

Deep mapping is part of the archaeology of the contemporary past.

Context

'Wooster Group pieces are rooted in the articulation of different kinds of performance space. In their evolving ecology of theatre, the kinds of spaces most used are:

Indoors:
House
Tent
Hotel room (usually Miami)

Outdoors:
Sea
Backyard
Highway (the Wooster Group has developed its own version of the "road play")

Media spaces:
Film
Video
Phonograph
Tape player
Photograph
Computer'

In Bonnie Marranca (2003) 'THE WOOSTER GROUP: A Dictionary of Ideas', *PAJ*, pages 4–5.

Space and Audience

Task

If the performance you are experiencing right now were in a **house**, what would be performed on the ground floor?

If the performance you are experiencing right now were in a **tent**, how would you first encounter it at dusk?

If the performance you are experiencing right now were in a **hotel room**, what would you hear through the thin walls from next **door**?

If the performance you are experiencing right now were at **sea**, which flag would you fly from the International Code of Signals?

If the performance you are experiencing right now were in a **backyard**, whose bones would you now be standing over?

If the performance you are experiencing right now were on a **highway/motorway**, who would pull up to your bumper baby?

If the performance you are experiencing right now were on **film**, what would the lead female whisper to her female sidekick?

If the performance you are experiencing right now were on **video**, which bit would you watch over and over until the image degraded into grey static?

If the performance you are experiencing right now were on a **phonograph**, where would you place the needle?

If the performance you are experiencing right now were on a **tape player**, what would you fast-forward through?

If the performance you are experiencing right now were on a **computer**, what would you delete from your hard drive?

Tasks: Audience

Found Movement

Watch for the repeated patterns located in the bodies of others. Steal their tics, absorb, make them yours, and then choreograph a response.

Tasks: Audience

Dear Audience,

If your audience practice were a city...

Task

Draw a city, including infrastructure, which describes your audience experience so far.

So if your audience practice were a city...

Where are your suburban and satellite areas as opposed to your distinct urban centre (material that you are comfortable with as well as that which is edgy and more dangerous)?

Where are your canals (dark waters), multistorey car parks (built on good and familiar foundations), botanical gardens (places of light)?

Do you Park 'n' Ride (anything you leave behind as an audience member)?

Do you have a pet name for Audience City (affectionate or not)?

Where is your zoo (places of monkey business), your museum (more traditional aspects of theatre), your big theatre (popular performance), your small theatre (weird shit)?

Where is your ring road (round and round in circles), your business park (serious stuff), your small airport (what makes you fly), your edge-of-town Hilton Hotel (sleep on it)?

Is there a section of town where nobody in his or her right mind would be wandering around after 10 p.m. (scary stuff)?

Tasks: Audience

Notice how the light falls through space

If the opportunity arises, ask, "what's the light like here in
[insert place name here]?"

Tasks: Audience

Dear Audience,
We have been
thinking about what
you might need
to build your own
'Audience Survival
Kit'. It should
probably have
sustenance, things to
keep you occupied,
and maybe a 'get out
of jail free' card.
Have a look at our
list, then see if you
can do better.

Bests
        Bob & Lee

Our Audience Survival Kit...

a glass vial for the collection of tears
a packet of Polo mints
headphones with music of your choice to block out
the difficult parts
Sunday best socks
clean underpants
a packet of tissues
permission to pay more attention to the motes of
dust in the lights than the things actual happening on
the stage
laser pointer
a comfy seat/a sturdy wall
the right kind of shoes
the right kind of coat
the right kind of laughter
back seat for theatre / front seat for cinema
rapt attention / complete disinterest
the willingness to share an armrest
a banana
a mirror (to check your face, or look at the people
behind)
cold hands/warm heart
a smile in the dark
an empty bladder

Tasks: Audience

Beginnings

Beginnings are easy. They're full of grand gestures and winks at the camera. They're all about pulling you in, inviting, enticing. Making you welcome. We can do beginnings with their eyes shut. We have a great track record with beginnings. We've started more things than it is possible to finish.

And here we are again. Back at the beginning, smiling and holding out a hand.

LIST 100 BEGINNINGS

Tasks: Audience

Aristotelian narrative arc:

It starts: we sit in a deserted restaurant and speak to our strange dead relatives as they form an orderly queue.

It ends: they count and name the bones in their feet, one by one, whilst rehearsing drunken soft landings.

Something from the middle: A Short List Found in Her Pocket …

1. We've explored all the corners but one.
2. We've placed our ears to the ground.
3. We've avoided all their handshakes.
4. I've lost you and found you again.

What are your beginning, middle and endings of a performance that will never be performed?

Write them down. Place in an envelope.
Lose between the pages of a book you'll never read.

Tasks: Audience

Observe. Take notes. Write the experience.

Tasks: Audience

Dear Audience,
Exploring habitus

Task

During the next week, we would like you to find one site that articulates a strong sense of habitus. 'Habitus' is a term used by the French sociologist Pierre Bourdieu to describe individuals' behaviour in space through a consideration of unspoken social and cultural interactions.

We want you to devise and document an intervention into space that resists habitus.

Lie down and sleep in corridors.
Spend time at a motorway service station, but never travel the motorway.

We're asking you to use your body as a means to challenge habitus.

Think carefully about what you place there, and the documentation, and remember that the rule that applies in quantum mechanics equally applies in sited work; if you observe it, its behaviour will change.

Pierre Bourdieu (1994 [1984]) *Distinction: A Social Critique of the Judgement of Taste*, translated by Richard Nice (London: Routledge).

This task allows you to resist categorisation, something that is not-theatre, not-art, not-dance, not-film. Something, in other words, that allows you to do what you want to do in your chosen space.

Tasks: Audience

Curate some properties

A chair
A coat
Some fuel
A book
A light
Something organic
Something alive
Something dead
Five things that mean nothing to you

Tasks: Audience

Assemble a cast

Some people, as many as you like, but more than one.
Perhaps you have dragged people in off the street.
Perhaps you have cultivated a group ethos. Whatever.

Tasks: Audience

Create a soundtrack

Nothing ever said above a whisper, music is fine, but lyrics fuck me off. Maybe a beat from a metronome, maybe a beat from a drum, maybe something else.

Tasks: Audience

Try all the doors you can see and go in.

Tasks: Audience

Disciplining the mind is as much a part of preparing
to resist as preparing the body. Finding ways to pay
attention to what is around you and to the way your
environment impacts upon your thought processes
is a big part of performance. It is important to allow
your embodied responses room to resonate. How
you feel in a given space is important, but so too is
why you might be feeling this way. Our bodies are
products of the culture they inhabit, acculturated
from early childhood. But the rules and regulations of
society also speak to the dominant hegemony. They
articulate power and control over the masses. Being
able to tune in to how you feel about something is
going to help you resist making knee-jerk, poorly
thought through responses. Think about developing
proactive, not reactive, responses to social, cultural,
and spatial stimuli.

Tasks: Affect

Dear Audience,
Helps

Ask me where it began

Ask me to do my party price

Ask me to sing a song

Ask me to hold you

Ask me look into your eyes

Ask me to make you a cake

Ask me for the world

Ask me for the truth

I'm sorry....

That is asking me too much.

The Qualic Exchange

A small girl wanders into the empty white room. There is something unsettling about her gait: she walks on the balls of her feet, not quite on tiptoe, but neither is she fully balanced. Her arms are held out in front of her. She moves them as if she can feel the texture of the air she is passing them through, as if this experience is a novelty. The girl is about seven, or nine, or maybe ten. On a couple of occasions she is nearer to twelve, but that version doesn't come out too often.

After a few long moments of watching her own arms swim in the air before her, her eyes come into focus and she sees the people in the room. She moves uncertainly towards me. The uncertainty is all physical: there is no reticence in the eyes. She looks for all the world as if she were made this morning: newly minted and still finding her edges, working out the limits of her capabilities. She moves towards me, looks into my eyes, but at the last moment shifts her gaze to the woman beside me. This is a strategy I will see her employ countless times over the next few days.

Her body facing me, her head turned to the woman beside me, she opens her mouth: 'Hello, I'm Ann Lee.'

Her voice has a slight mid-Atlantic quality. It doesn't quite feel like a well-travelled voice, a voice with the edges rounded off through hours spent on planes; rather, it feels like a voice that has spent too many hours in front of the TV. Too many hours of *The OC*, too many hours of *One Tree Hill,* too many hours of *Party of Five.* But that can't be the case. This body, the seven-year-old version, the nine-year-old version, even the more rare twelve-year-old – they haven't been in the world long enough to make these encounters.

As I listen, I hear more. Oldham, Prestwich, Didsbury, Bramhall, Bury: this voice is from around here, from lots of places around here. So why do I feel like it's from somewhere else at the same time?

I have no more time to reflect upon this, because her head has turned back to me, and she's asking me a question.

'Would you rather feel too busy or not busy enough?'

I don't know how to answer her. I want to be honest, and the honest response is not an either/or. I want to tell that it would depend on why I'm busy. Are these things I have chosen to do, or are they things given me to do, part of the overwhelming wave of shit that people ask me to do in order to justify their jobs/sense of self/existence? I'm aware of a bitterness in that response, and it doesn't offer the nuance of how I feel, anyway.

Her eyes continue to hold mine, filled with infinite patience. But the other eyes in the room, the ones who haven't been asked a question yet, don't look so relaxed. There is a hunger there, a need for someone to respond. I choke out a feeble, 'Not busy', and within seconds, I move for the exit. Over the next few hours, the next few days, I see this strategy played out across a number of other spectators. Over time, my own responses are sharpened, and I become more practised in my response, more able to hear the question, better able to offer a response that feels truthful in some way.

When she turns to a young man in the space and asks him, 'What's the relation between the sign and melancholia?', there is a palpable intake of breath. The room seems to grow smaller, contract in on itself as it waits for the answer, any answer. Eventually, the young man's small voice offers what is probably the closest thing to a collective thought I have ever experienced. He looks at her and quietly states, 'Honestly, I don't know.'

Ann Lee's response allowed the breathing to begin again: 'Okay. Take care.'

With that, she left. She always leaves.

* * *

This was our experience of encountering Tino Sehgal's Ann Lee in the *11 Rooms* exhibition, a series of body-based live performance and fine art practice installed in Manchester Art Gallery for the 2011 Manchester International Festival. Subsequently, the work was taken to the 2013 Frieze Art Festival in New York and has continued to tour internationally, with a further version being installed for the Berliner Festspiele in 2015. For us, *Ann Lee* offered a very particular understanding of Heidegger's consideration of boundaries. First, we are in a well-lit gallery space. The normal physical markers of live performance have been shifted somewhat.

Of course, in and of itself, this is nothing new; the physical demarcation of the fourth wall, a wholly appropriate artefact of the naturalist turn, has been roundly challenged by a range of performances practitioners over the last century.

Certainly, our experience of Tino Sehgal's *Ann Lee* offered just such a gap into which our spectatorial experience fell. *Ann Lee* is a live performance installation which, on the surface at least, offers a meditation on ownership and appropriation. It developed out of the work of French artists Philippe Parreno and Pierre Huyghe, who had in turn repurposed a character which began its life as a piece of anime from a Japanese development house. Once they had bought the image rights, Parreno and Huyghe used Ann Lee in their piece *No Ghost, Just a Shell* (2002). Playing on the title of the seminal *Ghost in the Shell* (a 1995 anime, which is itself an adaptation of the manga comic by Masamune Shirow about a female cyborg), Ann Lee was a stock character from the Japanese company K-works, which develops 'manga figures for animated films, comic strips, advertising, and video games' (Tanner, 2002: unpaginated). Following her acquisition by Parreno and Huyghe, she became a character shared amongst a loose artistic collective who brought her to life across a variety of animated platforms (see Tanner, 2002).

Even before the installation by Sehgal, Ann Lee's 'life' was a storied one: her animation by a range of artists resulted in a notoriety, if not a mythic status, as a hive of artistic activity centred upon this simple character originally bought by Parreno and Huyghe for $428USD (Tanner, 2002). Following that initial purchase, she was traded and lent rather than bought and sold, allowing her to function as metaphor for a range of artists across a variety of media. Thus the various Ann Lees of Sehgal's live performance installation inherit and build upon an existing multiplicity, as they are brought to life by a range of performers from the United Kingdom and the United States.

When trying to describe the various iterations of this character initially drawn from the pages of a Japanese trade catalogue, it is hard to find ways to describe her subsequent iterations without falling back on the word 'life'. The idea of this 2D figure being 'brought to life', or 'given life' by a range of artists even before the emergence of a live performed version, points toward the transformational aspect of what the artists felt they were doing with the base material of the 'bland, commercially produced cartoon drawing of a wide-eyed, elf-eared, prepubescent girl whose only distinguishing characteristic is her undeveloped potential' (Tanner, 2002: unpaginated).

There is little doubt that the variety of exchanges through which Ann Lee is given voice evoke questions as to how value is placed on life. In many respects Ann Lee is the perfect iteration of Irigaray's critique of 'exchange value'. Her worth is not measured in her accomplishments, but in the fact that she can be seen:

Woman takes pleasure more from touching than from looking, and her entry into a dominant scopic economy signifies, again, her consignment to passivity: she is to be the beautiful object of contemplation. (Irigaray, 1985: 26)

And once she has been seen and positioned as part of the scopic economy, she can be traded because

a woman is traditionally a use-value for man, an exchange value among men; in other words, a commodity. As such, she remains the guardian of material substance, whose price will be established, in terms of the standard of their work and of their need/desire, by 'subjects'. (Irigaray, 1985: 31)

It may seem somewhat reductive to invoke Irigaray here, but her critique of the consumption of women is a helpful reminder of the larger ideological implications for the casual trading that has occurred throughout the many iterations of *Ann Lee*.

Sehgal's resurrection of *Ann Lee* through the positioning of a series of 'real' girls in a 'real' gallery space, makes explicit the implications of ownership and trafficking that haunted her past. Indeed, the Internet terminology that sees a shift from virtual to real, often uses the term 'meatspace' to describe the non-virtual as a strategy to resist the real/not-real, and it is hard not to see these exchanges of the various Ann Lees as a commodity; a further indication that Ann Lee has been repurposed and in so doing explicitly become something to be weighed, measured and ultimately consumed.

In the previous section we explored how the intersubjective in-between allows for the development of an affective response to performance material. In this section, we hope to use our experience of *Ann Lee* to ask questions about what might be happening if the intersubjective seems to be lacking, and to consider what other ways performance work might be encountered. To this end we will consider the importance of absence and presence, and begin to open up questions about the role played by uncertainty in affective states. We have chosen to focus specifically on Sehgal's *Ann Lee* because it is a piece that has helped us to surface some of our questions about those moments in performance that we are coming to recognise as acts of transformation. Of course, those moments in between would be of much less import were it not for the knowledge that *Ann Lee* was a multiple, a composite persona long before Sehgal's work was realised. But it is with this knowledge of the already weighted sense of the transitions between various 'Ann Lees' that something of significance happens. Evidently, for those who did not witness the departure of one *Ann Lee*, the arrival of another marks the beginning of the installation. But for those who did witness this transition, those who experience the strange tabula rasa, what is to be made of the explicit sense of transformation which sees the interaction between one understanding of *Ann Lee* overwritten by another? The transformation referred to here is not the obvious transformation that inevitably occurs when one performer is replaced by another, but a shift of a rather more fundamental order. This is the transformation that happens as the *you* you know meets the *her* you don't, allowing for a chimeric shudder to unsettle one's stable sense of self.

Over the course of those three days in Manchester, we were witnesses to a variety of 'Ann Lees', and it was in the shifts between performers, where one *Ann Lee* left, and after a brief pause, another entered, that the work began to take on a significance for us. In his account of the New York version of the piece, installed in Marian Goodman's Frieze Booth, Andrew Russeth recalls the moment *Ann Lee* speaks of her inception:

> 'There were two artists—Pierre and Philippe,' the girl said slowly and confidently, gazing from one of us to the other. She had an otherworldly presence, as if she were speaking from some very nearby dimension, just out of reach. 'They were nice, and they seemed very busy.'
>
> [. . .] She told a story about visiting the home of Mr. Sehgal—also very busy as he talked on the phone—and finding a quotation in a book, which she recited. [. . .]

'I'm not sure what it means. Do you know what it means?' Two quick embarrassed head shakes from her audience.

'I can repeat it for you,' she said warmly.

She marched across the room, arms slightly akimbo, and repeated herself: 'Thus we ask now: even if the old rootedness is being lost in this age, may not a new ground and foundation be granted again, a foundation and ground out of which human's nature and all their works can form in a new way even in the technological age?'

She looked at us, and waited a few seconds for an answer. 'Okay, take care,' she said, and walked out, disappearing around a corner. (Russeth, 2013: unpaginated)

It is disappearance that leads us to consider those unspoken moments of magic that lead to emotional affect and those moments of disappearance that led to the impact of *Ann Lee* through the various Ann Lees. To be more specific, it was in those moments of transformation, where one girl becomes another, that our spectatorial struggle occurs. How are we meant to navigate the loss of one girl through the replacement of another? This is question that involves the head, the heart and the gut. At the purely cognitive level (if such a thing is possible), there was never any doubt that we were being asked to witness a singular entity, albeit one with multiple exteriors. Although that might well have been the cognitive response, the affective landscape, the one that accepts Brennan's psychoneuroendocrinological understanding of affect, positions these girls as avowedly different while also being identical. A certain cognitive dissonance results from such an experience, seeing individuals as both singular and multiple in the same moment. There was another question emerging with each transformation: just how many of these girls are there?

The initial question is innocent enough, coming as it does from a fairly mundane bit of conjecture. But as the various Ann Lees kept changing, a second question began to emerge: where is he getting them all from? It is in this moment that the 'reality' of the flesh collides with the 'fiction' of the piece (curiously in the typing of this sentence, the autocorrect function replaces 'collides' with 'colludes', and in truth either of these words would be wholly appropriate). It was in this moment of interchange that the work began to blossom: questions around trafficking became unavoidable, the role of these men in the easy and undisturbed exchange of a girl (albeit a fictional one), the exchange of monies, the exchange of ownership, the extreme and explicit objectification of something so incredibly autonomous, the sadness of Ann Lee's need to please the men who had bought, their ultimate rejection of her as she outgrew her use value whilst keeping some exchange value, and ultimately our complicity in this transaction. The awkwardness of the interchanges became more than understandable; they became a vital moment of witnessing our complicity and our inability, or unwillingness, to do anything for this evidently lost and confused child. It was in the moments of departure, in the periods where one Ann Lee transformed into another, that the space for discomfort began to emerge.

Perhaps this discomfort was due in part to the fact that the transformation occurring before us was not always about becoming; sometimes it felt more like an undoing, as if the manifold variants of this singular figure were washing out the colour from the bodies before us. It was in these moments between, the moments in which presences and absences were stretched, where time was attenuated and extended to the point that it felt as though we could sit inside them, that we were undone. At the end of the three days, we had become somewhat used to the discomfort and had begun to find some ease in our spectatorship. But as we walked away, something felt unresolved, as if the space in between us and the many versions of *Ann Lee* had released us into a continually unfolding space, untethered and unnervingly adrift.

Ann Lee returned to us in 2015, or maybe we returned to her – it's difficult to know which way it happened. What is sure is that our meeting was by accident, not by design. We were both in Berlin, working with some PhD students, when we heard there was a Tino Sehgal retrospective in the Martin-Gropius-Bau. This 'returning' was doubly so for us, having seen Sehgal's *Ann Lee* in Manchester, although we were not sure which pieces we were going to encounter before we entered each gallery room. Little could be gleaned from the programme notes, which read:

Tino Sehgal is regarded as one of contemporary art's most important pro-
tagonists. He constructs situations instead of material objects. His media are
the human voice, physical movements and social interaction. In this large scale
solo exhibition in Berlin, Sehgal will show five of his works.

These five performance scores, or 'situations' as Sehgal prefers,
were presented on the ground floor of the Martin-Gropius-Bau in
Berlin and interpreted through a cast of around eighty bodies who
shifted in and out of performance modes. As with the *11 Rooms*
gallery exhibition in Manchester City Art Gallery in 2011, there was
no opportunity to reference promotional or instructional material
that might serve to orientate the audience within Sehgal's work: no
posters, no photographs, no exhibition catalogue, no text and titles
mounted on foam core, no explanatory press release, and as Schaub
suggests, Sehgal's practice 'does not begin with the work, but rather
with its evasion' (2015: 272). This insistence on disappearance and
the tendency to evade is exemplified in the documentation of Sehgal's situations for dOCUMENTA(13) in Kassel. When searching
for Sehgal in the catalogue's index, readers are directed to page 159.
Upon searching they will find that page 158 is not immediately followed by page 159; indeed, page 159 cannot be found anywhere else
in the catalogue. The idea of disappearance is woven into the manner in which Sehgal makes his work, as he states:

> I don't make photographic or filmic reproductions of my work, because it
> exists as a situation, and therefore substituting it with some material object
> like a photo or video doesn't seem like an adequate documentation. Also, my
> works take a form that exists over time – as they can be shown over and over
> again – so they're not dependent on any kind of documentation to stand in
> for them. (Sehgal, in Griffin, 2005: 2)

In Schneider's terms Sehgal occupies that precarious position where he
upsets the 'logic of the archive' (Schneider, 2012: 63), because as Mary
Richards observes, 'No material evidence of Sehgal's work officially
exists' (2012: 72), causing Claire Bishop to wonder whether in time
the insistence on 'oral conservation [will] eat the works into oblivion?'
(Bishop, 2005: unpaginated). Sehgal creates fictions which cannot
exist outside of the immediate experience of their encounter: no photographs, no catalogues, no videos. His is a denial of the archive.

His refusal to offer any kind of steer does something interesting
to the audience, and our experience of re-encountering the work

resulted in something of a disjuncture as we pondered the mental arithmetic of fixing our mental images, calculating the ways to remember the experience. Helpfully, Sehgal has offered some thoughts on how the spectator might dwell on and in his practice, noting that '[i]t is really important for me to recall that our oral culture of remembrance is still the most powerful instance of knowledge transfer in our society today' (Sehgal, in Moehrke, 2011: 116). Throughout our time in Martin-Gropius-Bau, we both clung tightly to our notebooks, and it soon became clear that ours were not the only pen and paper in the gallery; small notations and drawings were constantly being made and added to by others, and as we caught the eyes of other scribblers, there were small smiles of recognition.

Sitting in the gallery's central space, a glass-ceilinged room which in high summer earns its nickname, Lichthof (Light Court), we encountered the first piece. *Kiss* (2007) appears at first blush to be a piece of gently looping contact improvisation, but over the course of the work its choreographed nature began to assert itself. In it, a female performer and a male performer make their way through a series of stylised clinches, some seeming to reference other embraces from art history, others belonging to the present moment. The Lichthof functioned as something of a receiving space, allowing the audience to orientate themselves but also potentially to decompress from the rooms that surrounded it. *Kiss* encouraged a gentle engagement, allowing as it did for the audience to look away, using moments of bashfulness as an excuse to disengage for a moment. Because there was no programme, and because we had chanced upon the exhibition without first going online to read reviews or blog posts, we had no sense of what was happening in the various spaces that radiated out from the Lichthof. As a result of this unknowing, Ann Lee would be the last piece we encountered. After *Kiss* (2007) we moved towards *This Variation* (2012), possibly because this was the room with most noise coming out of it. Moving out of the Lichthof, the Light Court, the space which housed *This Variation*, appeared to be pitch-black. Of course, this was a literal trick of the light, and as our eyes became accustomed to the gloom, we could see the performers scattered through the space, clapping, singing, humming. And as we got used to the darkness, we became aware of how ridiculous we must have looked, stumbling in, still blinded from the Lichthof, waving our arms before us, looking for all the world as if we were playing a solo game of blind man's bluff. At one point, the lights came on, just for a second, maybe not even a second. This happened whilst everyone was still in motion, still singing, still clapping. This might have been part of the 'situation', or it might have been an accident. This surprising burst of light unsettled the room for a while, exposing as it did those audience members who felt emboldened by the cover of darkness, and had used it as an opportunity to sing and clap along, exposing the joyful confusion of roles that the darkness allowed for.

Our next move was to cross the Lichthof to encounter *This Situation* (2007). This was the hardest room for us to stay with, probably because it made us feel very English. The work was a conversation in German between a group of six men and women. Theoretically this work is presented with a translator, but for the period we occupied the room, the conversation was undertaken entirely in German. It soon became clear that Lee's General Certificate of Secondary Education (GCSE) language skills were not enough to help navigate this piece, and the usual social anxiety we suffer from when travelling kicked in. Our lack of a second language is a constant cause of shame, and rather than sit with that experience, we quickly fled into the next room over/back out into the Lichthof to watch, *Yet Untitled* (2013). This was a piece in which the play of light and shadows across the space informed the solos, duets and small group choreographies, all played out in slow motion to gentle a cappella singing, soft beat-boxing and a series of percussive mouth sounds. As we moved back into the Lichthof, we watched this central space morph from an encounter of subtle intimacies to a large-scale interactive choreography. At least the small children occupying the gallery considered it to be interactive, and their energy, combined with the expert choreography and playfulness of the performers, transformed what had been, moments before, a sepulchral space into a party. We haven't been able to find the name of this piece, but when discussing the retrospective at the press night, Sehgal suggested that he would be installing five and a half 'situations' into the Martin-Gropius-Bau. Perhaps this large-scale playing was the half piece he referred to. Whatever it's name, it's impact was infections, and we carried with us this sense of elation as we moved into the final room, the room of Ann Lee.

It is really hard to write about our experience of *Ann Lee* in the past tense. There is something curious about the stasis of the memory that when we try to capture, when we talk through what we saw, we find ourselves telling each other what is happening, not what has happened. Neither of us is certain if this observation is significant, but we offer it here to explain the annoying shift in tense. We're sorry about this shift, but *Ann Lee* seems to resist memorialisation; she sits somewhere else, just above us, always out of reach.

There is something confusingly reassuring about coming into this space; it is empty as we arrive, and we move our way to the far side of the room and lean against the wall. As the first Ann Lee comes in, we sigh, relax and slide down the wall. It is unspoken: we both know we will be here for some time. She begins with a now familiar question: 'Would you rather be, too busy or not busy enough?' Except the familiarity is ours, not the room's. She asks the question three times, of three different spectators, until she elicits a response, and the response she gets is curious: 'Hmmm, interesting.' It is a response, but it is not an answer. Ann Lee is dogged, and she turns to Bob: 'Would you rather be too busy or not busy enough?' Bob wastes no time: 'Not busy enough, thank you.' Ann Lee makes her slow walk through the space, moving her arms as if they are suspended in water; she looks to the others in the gallery. A certain tightness becomes evident in the bodies of the other spectators, as if they are holding themselves in their unease. Looking around the room, there is sweat on upper lips; laughter too comes quickly through mouths held a little too wide.

The Berlin Ann Lees all have a similarity about them: with dark blonde, light brown mid-length hair. And they are young, maybe only nine. Like the voices of the Mancunian Ann Lees, there is a transatlantic slide to the delivery, but unlike their sisters from *11 Rooms,* this doesn't feel like a gloss, an affectation. There is nothing underneath the transatlantic drawl, no hint of regionality. These are the voices of Montessori children, used to speaking to adults; citizens of the world. The text feels familiar; we listen to it over and over again, hearing it loop through alternating Ann Lees. There is a curious doubling, from watching the text pass from Ann Lee to Ann Lee here in Martin-Gropius-Bau, but also because the text is looping from those bodies we used to know, those bodies that used to be in a gallery in Manchester. Listening now to their Berlin sisters (that's not quite right, they're not sisters, not really – unless they are like the 'sisters' from *Orphan Black*), there is that familiar rehearsed ease, not too scripted, but a reassuring contrivance.

It is becoming clear that in each of these retellings words and phrases remain the same, such as the fulcrum of the very last question. Asked directly into our faces, sometimes cornering and selecting one spectator, Ann Lee asks: 'What is the relationship between the sign and melancholia?' We watch as a number of spectators make their way through a range of responses. Mostly there is nervous laughter, muttered apologies, jokes about translation. Occasionally someone will make a concerted effort to meet the existential nature of the question, there is a pause and then a very earnest reply. But whatever reply is made to the question, it doesn't matter. Whatever is said, Ann Lee, all of her, just smiles, and offers the same response, always the same, always in that sad, dismissive tone, delivered over her shoulder, walking out of the room, leaving us with our own thoughts:

'Okay. Take care.'

After a few brief minutes, which usually correspond with the audience spilling out of the gallery room (even if they only caught the tail end of the Ann Lee performance), another Ann Lee enters with more questions: 'Where are you from?' and 'How are you?' The responses to these queries are barely registered as Ann Lee begins again, offering up her text, turning over the words like pebbles in her mouth, weighing the meaning of the words throughout. She stops on the word 'incorporated' and gently muses to no one in particular, 'I like that word, don't you?' Whether this is a performance strategy, a means to pause or delay so that Ann Lee can gather herself, is unclear; there is no way of knowing. Watching the various iterations, in various countries, it is certain that these are not improvised performances, even if they do hold the space for uncertainty. And when one of the Berlin Ann Lees says with a smile, 'This is a bit like theatre, don't you think? Tino told me he really likes theatre,' it's very hard not to smile back at this knowingness, as a nine-year-old playfully nods towards the tension between live/ performance art and theatre.

The baseline of *Ann Lee* is interruption – interruption through the constant comings and goings of the audience, but also in the ever-changing form of Ann Lee, one leaving the space to be replaced by another. Watching *Ann Lee* so many times affords us the chance to play with how to be an audience. Sometimes we dare each other to jump in with an answer to one of her questions. Other times, we tune out the spoken text to focus in on her small, economic movements. We make sure we are front and centre, visible to this Ann Lee, scrutinising her to see if she recognises one of us, but we both agree that she doesn't; she is far too engrossed in the task before her, the bodies of spectators merely a constantly ebbing and flowing tide, disengaged even when she looks directly into our eyes. Gazing at her, wanting her to see us, not simply to look in our direction; the scopophilic opens up, and it is impossible not to be reminded of the original 'owners' of this girl.

Parreno and Huyghe's initial purchase of *Ann Lee*, 'rescuing' her from the obscurity of K-work's catalogues, allows them to resist the eventuality of her disappearance. But it begs the question whether her shift in status is any better than the obscurity she was otherwise guaranteed. Despite the fact that we have only ever encountered Sehgal's Ann Lee, it is difficult not to see her through the filter of Parreno and Huyghe: their curation of a young girl, filling her empty shell with ideas and manifestations, then passing her around between their friends. She is here in front of us, but she is still in Rirkrit Tiravanija's 8-hour film *Ghost Reader C.H.* (2002), reading the entire text of Philip K. Dick's *Do Androids Dream of Electric Sheep?* (1968). The reference to Ridley Scott's *Blade Runner* (1982) and its genetically engineered robots, called 'replicants', is inevitable. Is it that what gives license to all the adults in the room? Licence to scrutinise these small girls? She has agency and autonomy, given life by Huyghe and Parreno at the Miami Basel Art Fair in 2002, signing over Ann Lee's rights to herself, while somewhere else in the same exhibition she is 'dying', as Joe Scanlan created a DIY funeral ceremony for her, complete with a flat-pack IKEA coffin.

Whatever pleasure is available when looking at all of Sehgal's Ann Lees, it is freighted with the knowledge of her exchange, the constant empty promises that artists have made to her. It is inevitable that once you know all of the grubby narratives that surround her inception, it is impossible to look away. When Seghal's Ann Lee asks, 'What is the relationship between the sign and melancholia?', perhaps she is telling us something about the existential crisis suffered by the cipher. What is it that Ann Lee believes is being signified, and is she the signifier in question? When reflecting on his earlier work presented at Manifesta 4, Frankfurt, Sehgal observes that some people will look at my piece for hours, I've realised, and they're comparing the people. Every two and a half hours the shift changes, and they say 'but this person was doing it like this', and yes of course, there is always going to be interpretation, there cannot be an original. (Obrist, 2003: UP)

Sehgal's recognition that there cannot be an original reminds us that when we are encountering *Ann Lee,* we are witnessing a girl who is constantly standing in for others, a girl with no real past, no sense of a future. She stands in for all the other versions of herself, always pointing towards the something/someone somewhere else.

Perhaps there was something inevitable in finding *Ann Lee* so far from home. Except, of course, she is not the one who is far from home. Instead, she reminds us that we don't really belong. *Ann Lee* has always been stateless, lacking a fixed context in which to grow. She has been blown to the four corners, taking root wherever she can. Watching these Berlin Ann Lees, thoughts turn to the Ann Lees in Manchester, the Ann Lees grown in the city in which we were both born. Those Ann Lees will be much older by now, four years older, no longer Ann Lees anymore. Their status was temporary, hosts to a viral code that has transmuted, shifted and travelled. The Berlin Ann Lees are only the current iteration of this virus, sitting in bodies newly minted, soon to be abandoned.

Ann Lee is stateless, yes, but she is timeless too. Whenever she is encountered, she is always the same, even as we change. Her move to new flesh serves to remind us of our own mortality. *Ann Lee* is a thing of bits and bytes; she is data housed in a corporeal shell. When she needs to, she will shift to another host, like some kind of sad, benign parasite. She will continue to move across sites, maybe out of the corporeal and back to 2D, shifting and changing in perpetuity. Ann Lee lives in the cloud. The cloud is a drifting and diaphanous network, and '[l]ike the inaudible hum of the electrical grid at 60 hertz, the cloud is silent, in the background, and almost unnoticeable [. . .] It is just there, atmospheric and part of the environment' (Tung-Hui Hu, 2015: ix). Like all things cloud based, the hardware *Ann Lee* occupies is less important than the interface itself. She is always there, floating just above us, waiting to be installed.

But the cloud should not become the focus. In *A Prehistory of the Cloud,* Hu describes it as something which you are only able to see in the moment of looking away. To look for the cloud is to miss the point, like staring into the beam of the projector in a cinema: 'You can get as close as you want to it, but the blinding light won't tell you much about the film, and it may even be dangerous for your eyes; it certainly involves turning your head away and not watching' (Hu, 2015: xx). Perhaps trying to follow the shifts across all of the performers playing *Ann Lee*, whether in Manchester, New York or Berlin, is akin to looking into the light of the projector; it is to miss the point. We should not be looking for their differences or for their similarities; instead, we should be looking to ourselves. How do we hold her in our gaze, and what do we see looking back? To look for the network of Ann Lees will not reveal the outline of Seghal's intentions. He is not interested in completing or fixing this. It is only through staring at the fulcrum point of *this Ann Lee* that gives a purchase to the work.

When we left *Ann Lee* in Manchester, we felt untethered, adrift. But as we leave *Ann Lee* in Berlin, we realise this is not the sea, but the sky. We have been left to float into the ether, finding our way into the cloud space she occupies, knowing that as we navigate our material bodies through the world, she will continue to float over us, waiting till she is pulled back once more into the flesh of her bodies.

The cloud removes the need to think of Ann Lee in terms of absence or presence, to resist a binary understanding of our experience of this young girl(s) in a variety of contexts. Perhaps then it is helpful to think of ways in which a resistance of binaries have been conceptualised. As we considered in the previous section, one possible way in is through the writing of Jon McKenzie, who attempts to avoid binary oppositions (that which is performance, and that which is not) by instead offering three paradigms that form a large 'performance' site. These three models (organisational performance, cultural performance and technical performance) describe the discipline and practice of performance, though these are not without their problems. What is afforded by this remembering of McKenzie is the idea of the third way. This wish to find ways of resisting the dualistic tenor of the debate and potentially open up alternative models in line with McKenzie leads us to the idea of 'thirdspace' as articulated by Edward W. Soja. Itself a development of the writing of Lefebvre, thirdspace as articulated by Soja offers a way of resisting the tendency towards a perceived binary in thinking about space that seems to ossify into dualistic tendencies:

The geographical imagination, especially as it has developed within the spatial disciplines continues to be confined by an encompassing dualism, or binary logic, that has tended to polarise spatial thinking around such fundamental oppositions as objectivity versus subjectivity, material versus mental, real versus imagined things, things in space versus thoughts about space. (2000: 17)

He offers a taxonomy of space that includes 'firstspace' as perceptual space, the space that can be perceived as 'real' and 'secondspace' as a conceived space or referencing representations of space. Soja goes on to position 'thirdspace' as a potential strategy of resistance which 'must be kept radically open (and yes, openly radical) for its interpretative insights and strategic power to be grasped and practiced' (1996: 107).

Although there are spatial dynamics at play in the work considered here (how could there not be? We are dealing with the interplay between bodies after all), it is not spatially per se that is the locus of our consideration. Rather, our invocation of Soja comes from a desire to locate that in-between-ness and recognise it as a space of dwelling rather than of transit. It is this cloud-like dwelling that we experienced in Sehgal's Ann Lee. The extended moments in-between the various versions of Ann Lee were the moments in which she was very much both absent and present. As we have suggested, it is only at the point that she ceases to be physically present, as we await the next version to arrive, that the psychic drag of the piece caught up with us. This was in part because the performer had left the space but also because of the shift in spatiality. The departure of the performer resulted in our standing in a white cube space, devoid of any art, with no contextual information on the walls, just a collection of people awkwardly waiting (or departing, or arriving), the room shifting from a context of exchange to a context of stasis; we were in a holding pattern. In removing the art from the walls of Manchester Art Gallery for the duration of *11 Rooms*, the 'coming down' reveals a sudden lack of anchorage for an audience. As we stand waiting for another Ann Lee, the building becomes defined by its internal corners and sharp folds. Where the eye usually would catch on paintings and sculptures, there is no such distraction from its inside architecture. The whiteness of the walls becomes an element in the construction of meaning. In these lacuna, the fundamental role of the audience, to witness, is called into question. These gaps are not of the same order as scene changes; they do not fit within the normative conventions of performance; they are gaps into which expectation can fall, where the role of audience is undermined and the standardised behaviours explicitly challenged.

The processes of performance entangled in matters of practical benefit are similarly in a constant state of flux, attempting as they do to describe the exchange and flow between bodies. All this points to the rather obvious recognition that bodies and spaces might be significant in their co-authorship, a realisation that there is a conjoining of the roles of space and bodies in relation to absence, presence and affect. This opens us up to a consideration of the word that serves as the heading of this section, 'qualia'. What we hope will happen, following our lengthy reflection on Sehgal's Ann Lee, is to explore how qualia might function as a significant filter through which to approach these ideas. Before we get to the necessary explanation of the term, we would like to round out our thinking on absence and presence through a brief return to Schneider, who asks:

> If we consider performance as 'of' disappearance, if we think of the ephemeral as that which 'vanishes', and if we think of performance as the antithesis of preservation, do we limit ourselves to an understanding of performance predetermined by a cultural habituation to the patrilineal, West-identified (arguably whitecultural) logic of the archive? (Schneider, 2012: 63)

It is that disappearance that we are wrestling with, trying to find a way to understand what has been happening within these gaps. Schneider is not alone in this consideration, as some thirty years earlier theatre academic Herbert Blau suggested that 'in theater, as in love, the subject is disappearance (1982: 94), intimately linking live performance to an expectation of absence. We return here to the presence of Ann Lee, the nascent woman at the heart of this discussion. Recalling the memory of a small girl(s) in a small white room, and then the same/different girl(s) in a larger room, we realised that it was in the moments of her disappearance that she became most present to us. Possibly this is because when she was there, she was never really present, speaking through us rather than speaking to us. Although she looked us in the eye, addressed us directly and misquoted Heidegger (thus we ask now: even if the old rootedness is being lost in this age, may not a new ground and foundation be granted again, a foundation and ground out of which human's nature and all their works can form in a new way even in the technological age?), the questions she posed were never aimed at uncovering a response. Perhaps it is this failure to appear that ensured she was never felt fully absent either, even when out of the room, holding steady in her cloud space.

By now you will have probably noticed that we like tasks; you will have hopefully undertaken some of the ones we have already offered in previous sections. Tasks are not just something we set for other people; they are also the things we use to understand our own encounters. Sometimes we set them for each other; sometimes we find them and see how they help frame our thinking. It feels as if we have been writing this section with one specific task in mind, inexorably zeroing in on one specific performance score from the artist Nye Ffarrabas. Working under the name Bici Forbes, her score 'Become Invisible' has taught us more about presence (and its trace counterpart) in performance than perhaps anything else.

Become Invisible

(a) by hiding
(b) by divesting yourself of all distinguishing marks
(c) by going away
(d) by sinking through the floor
(e) by becoming someone else
(f) by concentrating so hard on some object or idea that you cease to be aware of your physical presence
(g) by distracting everybody else from your physical presence
(h) by ceasing to exist (1966)

With the recognition that Ann Lee operates in a constant, impossible state of disappearance, we are reminded of the closing of *Perform, Repeat, Record: Live Art in History*, in which Adrian Heathfield suggests that

> [p]erhaps we should no longer speak of presence and absence, since there is neither one nor the other, but the tireless movement between: the continuous flux of bodies with other bodies. No more talk then of a unitary or

self-coincident body. No integrities, but instead intensities of exchange and flow. (Heathfield, in Glendinning, Heathfield and Etchells, 2012: 615)

There is no singular here, no suggestion that the archive can hold traces, because there can be no activation without witnesses, and the archive resists the messiness and interruption of bodies. In this sense, performance can only exist when there is a spectator to engage with it; it exists in the space between said bodies and the fluxual nature of their engagement. Or perhaps it is better to give the final words to Ann Lee: 'I like art and the places it is shown.'

* * *

Heathfield's qualification of presence and absence provides a helpful strategy to resist the binary either/or that did little to ground our experience of Sehgal's Ann Lee. The resistance of the binary grows out of an urge to understand what is happening in the exchange between performer and audience, and how this might in turn lead to the generation of affect. What we are attempting to address here is the difficulty of capturing, linguistically or lexically, that which is experienced in the space between subject positions. Although Heathfield may wish to recognise the 'intensities of exchange and flow' as a means to capture the mutability of the looping nature of absence and presence, how might we conceptualise the similarly fluid exchange between subject positions in performance?

Given the exploration of intersubjectivity and its role in affective transmission in the previous section, this shift in approach might appear to communicate a dissatisfaction with the term on our part. This is not our intention. Nor do we wish to undermine or equivocate in any way. Rather, we hope to find a way to negotiate the complexity of the exchange when the roles undertaken are themselves in flux. When thinking of the specifics of Ann Lee, the nature of the exchange is complex because the roles are open to change from moment to moment. With Ann Lee we were never fully certain what we were witnessing, because the performer was absent as often as she was present. Further, the spectator could be repositioned as performer if she found herself on the receiving end of one of Ann Lee's gnomic questions, questions seemingly designed to expose as much as lead to any sort of genuine dialogue. The result is that as spectators we were forced to fully engage with ourselves and our own subject position, rather than allowing ourselves to focus upon a contemplation of hers. This remained the case both in those moments of her presence as well as the extended moments of her absence. In her absence, we found ourselves wondering if we still occupy the role of spectator when there is nothing left to see. And if there is nothing to hear, can we still be an audience? If defining one's own role is so charged, what then of the exchange between these already uncertain subject positions? We could ask similar questions of the interchange between Abramović and those sitting opposite her. If we accept that the role occupied by the audience is that of co-creator[1], where the presence of the spectator activates the artwork, the nature of the exchange is similarly open to question and resistant to clear definition. Of course, there is a significant 'if' in that sentence. Nonetheless, it is as a result of this recognition that we began to wonder if there is some need to offer a qualification of the term 'intersubjective'. If the subjectivities it speaks to are in question – whether we are positioning them as co-creative or challenging the potential they hold for autonomy, does the potential for exchange shift? While this section does not claim to offer a taxonomy of terms to cover all possible combinations of audience/performer interaction, it will open up the debate around the terminology available to capture experiences of exchange in performance, and consider terms that might help to communicate the complexity of the relationship between the audience and the performer, especially in those instances where roles are flexible and open to negotiation.

It seems safe to say that spectatorship does not have clean edges. As Peggy Phelan notes:

Something happens, but by the time we notice, it has begun without us. Thus our access to the beginning is necessarily incomplete, fragmentary. (2009: 342)

The act of watching is interrupted even before we begin to think about the presence of those we watch or those who we watch with. According to Phelan, it stutters to life and creeps up on us when we

---

[1] As we have discussed in the 'Audience' section, we are not fully convinced by this sense of 'co-creation', given that it opens up a range of questions about ownership and other ideologically charged questions.

are maybe not unaware, but certainly not fully prepared. Although there is little doubt as to the value of an understanding of inter-subjectivity in performance, when the subjective positions at play involve a fictional narrative, the territory is made considerably more complex. In such situations we may be encountering the humoral processes of the actor (literally smelling them out) but witnessing the affective states of the character she is playing. Given that the 'what' of the exchange is already complex enough, the addition of a further uncertainty regarding who is involved in the exchange only deepens the potential for confusion. The term 'intersubjectiv-ity', although not rendered redundant if one subject is positioned like a 'man to double business bound' (Claudius in Hamlet), is certainly problematised in any attempt to explicate what happens when the real and the fictive exist cheek by jowl. This section looks for ways that we might process and account for this multiplicity in the audience/performer exchange. In the previous chapter we discussed the potential offered by Brennan in her consideration of affect being transmitted at the humoral level, a potential which remains rich with possibilities for thinking differently about the sharing of affective states. In our exploration of Brennan and the transmission of affect, we touched briefly upon the infra-thin of Duchamp, pointing to the potential issues arising from the fun-damental uncertainty upon which the term is built. As we move on to explore the uncertainty of the space in between audience and performer, we find that we may in fact need to develop ideas such as the infra-thin, in order to find articulation for the potential confusion afforded by the addition of a fictional landscape in the process of exchange.

By building upon the intersubjective exchange, we intend to move towards an understanding that might capture something of the space in between audience and performer and those moments of affective transmission, experiences which might be both 'real' and imagined. As we do not wish to give primacy to that which is based on the 'truth' of a 'real' moment over the fiction of infelicity, we feel a term that captures this uncertainty might prove a helpful way to explore the experience of spectatorship. Performance is a context which is multiple, both real and imagined. There remains an uncertainty around how best to capture that which happens in the hinterlands of performance; by focusing on those moments in between audience and performer, a context where there is already the added strangeness of an encounter that is not fully real, but still experienced as real, the potential for affect and how it might emerge requires a different order of language.

Duchamp's infra-thin offers us a way to think about those confusing moments of exchange, but because it is a term which deliberately resists definition, we might need to look for other ways to begin to articulate the uncertainty that lies at the heart of an intersubjective exchange within performance. One way to begin is to start with a concept which frames the difficulty in moving towards language. By recognising that we may have experiences that are resistant to verbal communication, this legitimises the potential problem presented by language as a means to outline interior states. This brings us to the term 'qualia', a word that addresses the problematic nature of language, and points to those

> experiences, or at any rate properties of experiences that make it like something to have the experiences. They are what Herbert Feigl (1967) called 'raw feels', Thomas Nagel (1974) calls the 'subjective characters of experience' and David Chalmers (1996) calls 'phenomenal states'. (Perry, 2012: 251)

A quale is when the explicatory power of language is usurped by experience – when a gap opens up between the sensate and the cognate, a gap that cannot be bridged by lexical or linguistic means. Qualia are those occasions of singular and subjective consciousness, the 'raw feels' that let us know what it is to be. It is a term that allows for a recognition of the difficulty in articulating an experience. One of the most familiar ways to attempt to communicate qualia comes in the discussion of describing a sensation. Although we may all know conceptually what 'pain' means, we cannot begin to understand someone else's experience of pain; the experience is entirely subjective, and while we can offer an analogy to describe the experience ('it felt like red hot needles'), this is a translation of the experience through a mediating filter in order to make sense of the qualia, or the 'raw feels'. Although the analogous description might help the witness understand the sensation, the language cannot help him or her to experience it. One subject's experience will remain just that, a subjective experience. Any attempt to share it will simply be a narrative account. The gap between an experience and the articulation of said experience remains a territory fraught with uncertainty and debate. In his attempt to communicate how we experience qualia, Michael Tye asserts that

[o]ur grasp of what it is like to undergo phenomenal states is supplied to us by introspection. We also have an admittedly incomplete grasp of what goes on objectively in the brain and the body. But there is, it seems, a vast chasm between the two. It is very hard to see how this chasm in our understanding could ever be bridged. For no matter how deeply we probe into the physical structure of neurons and the chemical transactions which occur when they fire, no matter how much objective information we come to acquire, we still seem to be left with something that we cannot explain, namely, why and how such-and-such objective, physical changes, whatever they might be, generate so-and-so subjective feeling, or any subjective feeling at all [. . .] This is the famous 'explanatory gap' for qualia (Levine 1983, 2000). Some say that the explanatory gap is unbridgeable and that the proper conclusion to draw from it is that there is a corresponding gap in the world. (Tye, 2013: unpaginated)

The idea of a gap in the world is a seductive one, as it suggests that there might be words missing that speak to our experience, which in turn helps to position us as somehow unique, that there is still enough originality in existence to have avoided linguistic framing. In his overview of qualia, Tye suggests that qualia might be the tip of the iceberg when it comes to as-yet undefined, if not indefinable, states of mind. He asks:

Should we include any other mental states on the list? Galen Strawson has claimed (1994) that there are such things as the experience of understanding a sentence, the experience of suddenly thinking of something, of suddenly remembering something, and so on. Moreover, in his view, experiences of these sorts are not reducible to associated sensory experiences and/or images. (Tye, 2013: unpaginated)

Tye's use of Strawson, a critic and philosopher specialising in metaphysics, points to a world view in which the experience of cognition is complex and resistant to easy compartmentalisation; the assertion being that our experience of experience is a unique and messy affair, one that may not fall into an easy taxonomy. It is precisely this uniqueness that leads cognitive scientist and philosopher Daniel Dennett to offer a rather robust critique of qualia, which he summarises as 'supposed to be properties of a subject's mental states that are: (1) ineffable; (2) intrinsic; (3) private; (4) directly or immediately apprehensive in consciousness' (Dennett, 1988: 385). His take on the term 'qualia' is that its resistance to definition renders it functionally useless when trying to explicate interior processes. Central to his critique is that 'there is no agreed-on definition. This does not bother philosophers as it might be expected to' (Dennett, 2005: 78), and he continues that 'philosophers have endowed the term with a variety of ill-considered associations and special powers' (Dennett, 2005: 78), which evidently leaves him unsatisfied. When considering what definitions do exist, Dennett is clear that '[i]t also does not help us when we are told that qualia are what zombies don't have', articulating his understandable frustration over the evocation of a fictional existential state as an attempt to offer some form of explanation. Drawing from the thought experiment first propounded by Chalmers in his book *The Conscious Mind,* one way of explicating how qualia might function is through the imagining of a philosophical zombie. This zombie is of a somewhat different order to the filmic zombie[2] made famous in George A. Romero's *Night of The Living Dead.* Unlike its filmic counterpart, the philosophical zombie is not a reanimated corpse or a creature under the thrall of a spell. The philosophical zombie is a creature which to all intents and purposes appears and functions like any other human being, except that it lacks any conscious experience, or qualia. It can be injured and if so will communicate these injuries through normal processes (it will bleed, cry out, etc.), but significantly it cannot feel these experiences, so any outward signifiers of experience are merely performed. The philosophical zombie is behaviourally identical to the human, only without conscious experience. Chalmers suggests that the philosophical zombie

will be awake, able to report the contents of his internal states, able to focus attention in various places and so on. It is just that none of this functioning will be accompanied by any real conscious experience. There will be no phenomenal feel. (Chalmers, 1996: 95)

Perhaps the experience of watching Ann Lee is to witness a philosophical, or p-zombie in action, performing all the outward signifiers of emotion but unable to feel them, smeared as she is across

---

[2] See Miller's (2014) editorial introduction to *Studies in Theatre and Performance,* 34(3), for a more detailed discussion of the zombie.

multiple bodies and retreating to the cloud whenever she is unwitnessed. In many ways the p-zombie evokes the infelicitous performative of Austin, performing emotion or experience without any of the actual feeling. The difference though is that the p-zombie is a philosophical construct used (in-part) to explain qualia, whereas the actor of Austin is real, and the infelicitous action is not a thought experiment, but an action that may ultimately lead to the development of a 'real' sensation. We are not certain where this leaves *Ann Lee*, because she is *both* an actor *and* a thought experiment undertaken by Sehgal, Parreno and Huyghe et al., her roles already multiple and confused.

Dennett dismisses the p-zombie when he observes that it 'seems to be growing in popularity as a way of pointing to the elusive quarry, while [we await] a satisfactory definition' (Dennett, 2005: 79–80). For Dennett, the p-zombie is a stopgap measure at best, one which can only ever explain qualia within its own limited terms. It would seem that for Dennett if there is no consensus regarding the definition of qualia, the concept cannot usefully inform debates around selfhood. Qualia, those 'subjective characters of experience' (Nagel) fail for Dennett for exactly the reason they succeed for other theorists; it is their subjectivity, the avowedly interior which resists articulation, that is at the root of the problem, one that is made worse by subsequent attempts to articulate their resistant nature.

In some ways, Dennett's resistance to qualia is in direct contrast to the acceptance of the openness of the term 'performance' by scholars working within the field of theatre and performance studies. Terms which resist or in some way fail, are central to scholarship in the field of performance studies. Indeed, in the articulation of the term 'performance', it is often defined in part through its inability to be singularly classified:

> Performance, like art and democracy, is what W. B. Gallie (1964) calls an essentially contested concept, meaning that its very existence is bound up in disagreement about what it is, and that the disagreement over its essence is itself part of that essence. (Strine, Long, and Hopkins in Soyini Madison and Hamera, 2005: xi)

One reason that performance has been embraced is precisely because of its ambiguity. In this context, the use of 'qualia' as a means to define the impossibility of speaking the complex emotional and affective responses to moments in performance might not be the sloppy thinking suggested in Dennett's critique of the term, but more in keeping with the 'essentially contested' landscape in which these exchanges occur.

The fictional nature of the p-zombie leads us to return to the idea of infelicity and fiction. In the previous section we touched briefly upon Damasio's concept of the 'as-if' body loop, a process in which affective states might also be achieved through memory or imagination rather than occurring exclusively through experience. Damasio thus positions 'the body as a theatre for the emotions' (2006: 155), a conceptualisation that does not include the inherent critique of the theatrical implied by Austin, or by Dennett. The 'as if' of Damasio is of a significantly different order to those conceptual work-arounds that Dennett struggles with. For Damasio, the 'as if' is a proposition that, despite its roots in fiction, has an impact on the affective experience of the subject. Contrast this with the introduction of the p-zombie and other such deus ex machina intended to make the analysis of consciousness more coherent. It was a resistance to homuncular theories of cognition that led to the development of Dennett's multiple drafts of consciousness model, a counter to the Cartesian Theatre of the Mind, in which consciousness is envisioned as a theatre into which sensory experience is projected and subsequently watched and analysed by a miniature version of our physical self (the aforementioned homunculus). Here Dennett is offering the analogue of the theatre as a critique, which contrasts with the approach taken by Damasio.

Partly by accident, partly by design, much of the work we have reflected on has been either contemporary devised theatre or performance art. This isn't because we don't watch 'traditional' theatre, nor is it because traditional work falls outside of our field of interest. I suppose it has something to do with the fact that much of our debate has been focussed on work that is the seems to be explicitly engaged with generation. However, this runs the risk of us appearing to set up a binary in which traditional practice is precluded from conversations around the generation of meaning. We have no intention to create a false split which makes traditional audiences out to be passive, so I would like to tell you a story.

When I was eighteen years old, I went to see a play.

For Damasio, the invocation of the theatrical is not intended as a critique. Despite accepting the value in positioning 'the body as [a] theatre for the emotions' (2006: 155), Damasio's 'as-if' body loop moves beyond the need for theatrical analogy, while still keeping a connection to an imaginary landscape. If the body loop relies on the theatrical, the 'as-if' body loop moves beyond this analogy in a way that does not assume infelicity. Further to this, he does not seek to undermine the affective state achieved through such potential 'falsity' – if it is felt, it is 'real'. Any invocation of theatre reminds the reader that she can have 'real' emotions stimulated by fictional events. Indeed, much of Western theatrical product is based upon the assumption that Aristotle's cathartic experience through art is not only possible but actively beneficial. The 'fake-it-till-you-make-it' advice of self-help, has seen some supportive literature emerging from within the cognitive sciences[3], suggesting that physical postures can have a positive impact upon psychological states, which helps to further frame the looping nature of Damasio's assertion, suggesting as it does that the inner can affect the outer and, significantly, vice versa. Infelicity does not come into the debate; instead, efficacy is the primary driver. Damasio is not offering metaphor here; he is referring instead to the biology of the brain by recognising that

> the activation of neurotransmitter nuclei in the brain stem and their responses bypass the body, although, in a most curious way, the neurotransmitter nuclei are part and parcel of the brain representation of body regulation. There are thus neural devices that help us feel 'as if' we were having an emotional state, as if the body were being activated and modified. (2006: 155)

In this instance, the 'as-if' body loop does not require the body to become a theatre for the mind, where emotional states are played

---

[3] See J. D. Laird (1974) 'Self-attribution of Emotion: The Effects of Expressive Behavior on the Quality of Emotional Experience', *Journal of Personality and Social Psychology*, 29(4): 475–86; and J. Michalaka, K. Rohdeb and N. K. Trojec (2015) 'How We Walk Affects What We Remember: Gait Modifications through Biofeedback Change Negative Affective Memory Bias', *Journal of Behavior Therapy and Experimental Psychiatry*, 46(March): 121–25. Similar territories are explored by Amy Cuddy, whose 2012 TED talk was viewed more than 30 million times, giving it a ranking of the second-most-viewed TED talk at the time of writing.

out, as the body is bypassed altogether. Damasio does ask if these 'as-if' experiences are the same as those housed in the body, but he doesn't suggest that they are somehow less real; this is not a hierarchy of feeling, but merely a differing affective strategy. Damasio does not concern himself with metaphorical means to explicate the development of affective states, but instead considers their neurological roots.

The year was 1991, and I was an undergraduate studying for a degree in drama. I was attending a university in the North-West of England, and my year group were taken to see John Ford's *'Tis Pity She's a Whore* at the Swan Theatre, Stratford-upon-Avon. According to Google, this RSC production was directed by David Leveaux, and starred Saskia Reeves as the eponymous whore. I had to look that information up; it's been a while. I do remember that I was fairly excited to be going to see some theatre. It was my first trip to Stratford, and I had recently seen Reeves in the film *Close My Eyes*, so I was really looking forward to seeing a famous person. This might sound rather shallow, but I was an eighteen-year-old from Cumbria, and I didn't get out much.

Memory is a curious thing. I'm sitting here trying to recall experiences from over twenty years ago, from a time when I was an entirely different person. If, as L. P. Hartley would have it, the past is a foreign country, then our former selves are surely people who speak a different language from us. Trying to remember the sequence of events, the broader context of the trip, the people I sat with, the conversations we shared – all of this is lost to me. Dennett offers his 'multiple drafts' theory of consciousness, in which memories are not fixed, but 'smeared', overwritten by other tellings and re-rememberings. This might run counter to the more commonly articulated 'flashbulb' memory, in which a particularly vivid moment is fixed in consciousness.

To return to Dennett, as a means of explicating conscious thought, the homunculus throws up as many problems as it solves; is the projection being watched by a physicalised self who sits in the head of the homunculus to process what she sees, or are we to imagine

a never-ending line of matryoshka-like watchers, each smaller version nested inside the head of the previous one? Thus, Dennett's
resistance comes in the form of his multiple drafts model, in which
consciousness is made up of a smearing of experience through the
brain, rather than being housed in a singular theatre-like reposi-
tory. Ultimately Dennett is resistant to a dualistic understanding
of cognition, favouring instead the messiness of consciousness
being constructed in both a spatially and temporally extended
fashion, one which strongly resists the idea that subjective experience lies beyond the scope of objective consideration:

> [T]here are, however, some events that occur in my brain that I do know
> about, as soon as they occur: my subjective experiences themselves. And these
> subjective experiences, tradition tells us, have 'intrinsic qualities' – qualia, in the
> jargon of philosophers – that I not only do not have access to, but that are inac-
> cessible to objective investigation. This idea has persisted for centuries, in spite
> of incoherence, but perhaps its days are finally numbered. (Dennett, 2005: 78)

When held against Dennett's generally dismissive attitude towards
philosophy or Brennan's discussion of psychoneuroendocrinology
(see previous section), Tye's apparent capitulation to the mystery of
the brain/body split might seem like a return to a Cartesian positioning of cognitive and affective states being somehow untethered
from the physiological. Dennett's smearing, relying as it does on
visceral imagery, keeps conversations around consciousness avowedly connected to the physical. Of course, as one might expect,

---

I strongly remember the denouement, or more specifically the cognitive dissonance I felt as I watched it play out. The play ends with Giovanni having murdered his sister, Annabella, during an incestuous kiss
off stage. In the version I saw, he entered with her heart in his hand (in
the text, her heart is speared on his dagger) and walked to the front
of the stage. Even to this day I can never remember where the 'good'
seats in a theatre are supposed to be. Front, middle, dress circle, stalls –
I can never remember where I should sit. I know that then my seat was
very near the front; it might even have been on the first row – I don't
quite remember. But I do remember that something smelt wrong.
    It was the heart. It was Giovanni. Or rather it was both of them.

Tye himself is equally cautious about the propagation of a further unhelpful binary split as he attempts to make sense of qualia:

> There aren't two sorts of natural phenomena: the irreducibly subjective and the objective. The explanatory gap derives from the special character of phenomenal concepts. These concepts mislead us into thinking that the gap is deeper and more troublesome than it really is. (Tye, 2013: unpaginated)

Tye is no more keen to return to the brain/body split than is Dennett, and in many ways Tye's conceptualisation of cognition owes more to the thirding we see in the writing of Lefebvre and Soja (discussed above). Despite Dennett's dissatisfaction with the term 'qualia', for many it still offers a useful way to conceptualise the gap between experience and the ability to communicate said experience. While we are not entirely convinced that qualia points to a gap in the world, it almost certainly points to a gap in

Lying on the stage were two dead characters: one, Florio, had died of shock; the other, Soranzo, was mortally wounded by Giovanni. It is in the space between Soranzo and the heart that my memory is stuck. Giovanni and Soranzo had been involved in a fight before the fatal blow was struck, and the two performers had been running around the stage a fair bit. As I gazed at Soranzo's corpse, I was immediately aware of the rise and fall of his chest. The actor had been working hard in the fight choreography, and as he lay on the stage before me, his breathing was taking a while to return to a more routine rhythm. I could see the sweat staining his costume, and smell the heat coming from him. There is nothing unusual about this; he really was very, very near. But there was the heart.

What I am trying to articulate here is the unspoken rule of the willing suspension of disbelief; this is a perfectly normal theatrical convention, where we see one thing, but understand it to be another. The cloak of invisibility, the passing of time, the 'vacant air' that contains a character. The examples are manifold, part and parcel of the theatrical experience. And yet, the cognitive dissonance I experienced, the shock of two conventions colliding, in that moment short-circuited a given convention, resulting in me struggling to understand what was expected of me. In some ways, that moment led to the writing of this book (with many other moments along the way, joining all the moments that Bob has had).

the words, and it is the difficulty inherent in the term that leads us to adopt and adapt it to develop the intersubjective exchange between the performer and the audience. The term 'qualia' has been surfaced as an attempt to make sense of these subjective experiences and to consider how their irreducibility might inform the moment of subjectivity, where we are able to see, recognise and become ourselves. As such, qualia has emerged as a way in which philosophy has attempted to conceptualise the process of understanding one's interior processes. These moments of subjective conscious experience test the edges of how moments of interiority are conceptualised and communicated.

In performance, we would like to suggest that the uncertain space in between the performance and the audience can be framed as a qualic exchange. Fiegl's term 'raw feels' might helpfully locate the value of this qualic perception within the broader debate offered here as to how we might begin to understand that which passes between in the intersubjective exchange. Fiegl's use of the word 'raw' helps to conceptualise the lack of processing that the 'feels' have gone through. Like raw data, raw feels are unprocessed: they simply are. They have been felt, but haven't been through any further process of interpretation or communication. The raw feel is pure perception, free from any interpretation. In contrast, 'cooked feels' have been processed, and are thus considered in terms of their potential effects. The raw feel of pain is the sensation ('Ow!'); the cooked feel of pain is the potential implication of being affected by the pain ('Oh, I've been injured').

The understanding of pain is an excellent example of how raw and cooked feels. How pain is conceptualised and talked about has been the subject of enquiry in the fields of both arts and medicine. Deborah Padfield's project *Perceptions of Pain*, was a collaboration between the artist Padfield, Consultant Pain Specialist Dr Charles Pither and patients undergoing residential treatment at the St Thomas' Hospital INPUT Pain Clinic in London. Padfield recognised the limitations of numeric scales as a means to address and articulate the complexities of living with chronic pain. When a healthcare professional might ask a patient to register pain on a scale of 1 to 10, it was felt that the apparent universality of such a scale might confuse the patient trying to understand and explain his or her own experience. Instead of focusing on the experience patients might try to work out where they sat on the scale in relation to other patients. Working with patients in the clinic, Padfield produced images which were then developed into a pack of cards, with the intention to encourage patients to find ways to explore and record their experiences of pain: 'I can't feel the flesh properly, it is as if it were not alive, as if it had been turned off in some way (Pain sufferer)' (Padfield, 2003: 704). Padfield's cards facilitated communication between patients and clinicians which focused on articulating actual and personal sensations, and also explored assumptions about pain experience, both within and outside of the medical setting.

It is not just the exchange in the moment of performance that raises questions how best to communicate the nature of an experience. In his book *The Shadow of the Object: Psychoanalysis of the Unthought Known* (1987), Christopher Bollas introduces the term 'unthought known' as a means to conceptualise those experiences of which the individual is aware but unable to cognitively process or fully articulate. In this sense, the unthought known can be seen as a preverbal response to experience. The significance of preverbal thought in understanding the territory around qualia can be seen in Damasio's explication of the importance of social construction on selfhood:

> The picture that I am drawing for humans is that of an organism that comes to life designed with automatic survival mechanisms, and to which education and acculturation add a set of socially permissible and desirable decision-making strategies that, in turn, enhance survival, remarkably improve the quality of that survival, and serve as the basis for constructing a person. (Damasio, 2006: 126)

For Damasio, becoming a person entails a complex set of circumstances which require both biology and culture, as neural mechanisms 'require the intervention of society to become whatever they become, and thus are related as much to a given culture as to general neurobiology' (Damasio, 2006: 126). Given that language is an avowedly acculturated product of society, a shared system of meaning making, the idea of preverbal responses to experience as surfaced by Bollas weighs heavily in favour of the functional value of qualia. If there are potentially experiences which are felt, and come to consciousness in a prelinguistic fashion, an understanding of the potential issues presented by such a process is a valuable way in to thinking through affective moments, both in performance and beyond. Without language, how are Fiegl's 'raw feels' able to move outward? Damasio suggests that the processing through language is in itself a phenomenal act, one deeply embedded in the humoral state, and that 'the etymology of the word nicely suggests an external direction, from the body: emotion signifies literally "movement out"' (Damasio, 2006: 139). This outward-facing structuring of emotion allows Damasio to consider how emotions work within the structuring of the brain:

> [E]motion is the combination of a mental evaluative process, simple or complex, with dispositional responses to that process, mostly toward the body proper, resulting in an emotional body state, but also toward the brain itself. (Damasio, 2006: 139)

What is being spoken of here is a series of inward-focused processes, which resist comfortable or easy communication. These are moments of intimacy, designed to foreground interior processes. That they struggle to be translated into language, a culturally constructed and shared means of communication, merely reminds us of their intimate nature. The outward trajectory to which Damasio points, the motion to which he refers, starts in stillness, in silence. The 'raw feels' of interiority must be processed and cooked in order to be usefully shared. Dennett's resistance to qualia seems to come from it having been imbued with 'special powers' (Dennett, 2005: 78), a little like the mysticism we feel lies at the heart of the infra-thin. However, our intention here is to move away from the idea that qualia have magical qualities and instead see the term as a means to articulate the intimate, that which sits outside of the publicly facing discursive strategies of linguistic and lexical modes of communication.

The relationship between qualia and the unthought known has already been sketched out above, and this connection can also be traced through another psychoanalytic approach to understanding the self. Developed as a therapeutic tool intended to open up space for non-judgemental awareness of interior states, focusing was developed by Eugene Gendlin and relies on the cultivation of an awareness of the felt sense. Its non-judgemental approach shares territory with the relationship between the mover and the witness in *Authentic Movement* practices (as discussed in the section on audience), and the focusing on subjective sensations which have yet to be brought to consciousness through language also shares similarities with Bollas's unthought known, which in turn shares territory with qualia. For Gendlin, it was from an engagement with the felt sense that the therapeutic process could begin. In this respect it differs from the unthought known and qualia because there is the expectation that action will lead from the experience of recognising the felt sense. Each share territory because of their singular nature, as all are conceptualised as interior responses to subjective experience. The unthought known speaks to that moment before language, when we might feel something but have yet to know it. Similarly, the felt sense is understood to be something that we have to search for, a preverbal 'tickle' that must be deliberately sought out in order that it might transform from something unspoken to something that might be worked from and worked through.

In a bid to address the complexity of a performance-based exchange, we would like to offer the concept of the qualic exchange as a means to articulate what might pass between in the audience/performer dynamic. We consider the qualic exchange as a process which embraces the strangeness of an encounter that is not fully real, while allowing the potential for affect to emerge. Arguably it shares territory with the infra-thin, and while there are certainly echoes of this within the qualic exchange, we are not suggesting a simple equivalence. We do not offer the qualic exchange as an opportunity to fall into a 'gap in the world'; instead, we suggest that it might serve as a means to reflect upon those raw moments that pass between subjective positions in performance. The qualic exchange is an attempt to give value to the experiential in spectatorial practices; to recognise that sometimes we have experiences that we don't always understand, but that doesn't mean that we must ignore them. It is being positioned here as an attempt to recognise that an affective transmission can take the form of a quale, a genuinely felt moment that leads to psychological and physiological shifts, albeit changes that might resist transmission through language. If we cannot always explain to ourselves what we are feeling, how can we then hope to share that experience with another? If we allow qualia into the narratives of spectatorship, we might begin to find other ways to communicate our experience and develop deeper strategies for reflection. At the start of this section, we surfaced our concerns regarding the intersubjective and found that, particularly in the experiencing of Sehgal's *Ann Lee,* the term doesn't quite capture the exchange. If we are to move forward and to address the gap in the words, we require a different order of language. The qualic exchange seeks to develop the singular experience and to allow for the intimacy of the moment in-between in performance. It is distinct from intersubjectivity in the recognition of the inherently uneven relationship between audience and performer, and the potential for confusion that could arise from the fictional nature of the encounter. In earlier sections we have considered the potential for intimacy in performance, particularly in those more interactive modes of practice. It is important that we are clear to reinforce the continued potential for the intimacy of a qualic exchange. Even though there are potential gaps into which the experience might fall, and we have raised questions about the uneven nature of the exchange, this should not be mistaken as a disavowal of the potential for intimacy. Intimacy is always in potentia within a performance context, partly because of the overwhelming power of the imagination. It is through imagination that a specific form of intimate encounter in performance has emerged, an encounter which accounts for the apparent disparity in audience/performer dynamic.

The term 'para-social' refers to an uneven interpersonal relationship, in which one party will have significantly more information about the other. The experience, while not one-sided as such, is certainly uneven. Although we are not trying to articulate a perceived hierarchy in performance exchange, we do wish to acknowledge that the space which opens up between performer and spectator differs from the intersubjective experience of daily practice. Typically, this unbalance occurs between a celebrity and a fan but can also be extended to the relationship between an audience and a fictional character. The term was introduced by Donald Horton and Richard Wohl in their paper 'Mass Communication and Para-social Interaction: Observations on Intimacy at a Distance'. Written in 1956, the paper explores the emergence of then new forms of mass-communication, with a particular emphasis being placed upon the emergence of television in US culture. The opening sentence of the paper states that '[o]ne of the striking characteristics of the new mass media – radio, television, and the movies – is that they give the illusion of face-to-face relationship with the performer' (Horton and Wohl, 1956). They argue that it is this sense of intimacy, informed by the shift in performance modality ('often [the actor] faces the spectator, uses the mode of direct address, talks as if he were conversing personally and privately' [Horton and Wohl, 1956]) that allows the para-social to emerge. Significantly for our argument is the following assertion:

> The crucial difference in experience obviously lies in the lack of effective reciprocity, and this the audience cannot normally conceal from itself. To be sure, the audience is free to choose among the relationships offered, but it cannot create new ones. (Horton and Wohl, 1956)

In 2016, the performance and media landscape is somewhat different in terms of reciprocity and interactivity. Whereas in 1956, the context was one of mass-media broadcasting, for the viewer in 2016, there is an increasing and significant shift towards narrowcast and on-demand engagement with media content. The principle of broadcast networked TV has been gradually eroded by new technologies, with YouTube channels curated by on-screen personalities responsible for their own content generation (PewDiePie, Zoella et al.), allowing for a much clearer space for interaction. Mainstream broadcasting has learned from this narrowcast approach, and includes texts, tweets and phone-calls within their programming. Of course, we are evidently referring here to the types of output which foreground direct address, and trades in veracity of experience, however ersatz that 'truth' might be. That said, the overall landscape of interactivity might be seen as having allowed the para-social to become a more deeply embedded cultural trope. In the first section of this book (Audience), we discussed James McQuaid's anxiety over the potential confusion caused by the emergence, and growing significance, of user-generated content. His thesis considered the potential move towards amateur cultural product impacting negatively upon the wider arts environment. As we noted, this bespeaks an entrenched them/us binary which might not be entirely helpful when exploring strategies of co-creation. Significantly, the reinforcing of a binary position ensures that a hierarchical reading of performer/audience dynamics is inscribed. User-generated content has the potential to shift the expectation around engagement significantly, explicitly allowing for the development and renegotiation of para-social interactions. Such shifts allow for relationships that are not merely imagined, but potentially 'real' through the use of direct contact between makers and audience.

It is this shift towards a para-social understanding of the performer/ audience dynamic that results in us trying to find a more nuanced way to articulate the intersubjective exchange. A qualic exchange, as we are beginning to surface it here, describes the inherent oddness of the moment of intimacy between two strangers. This might result in what Buber calls an 'elemental togetherness' (Buber, 1937: 86), an exchange which is deeply affective but which cannot quite be articulated.

It is necessary here to express the value of recognising the para-social in a qualic exchange; it is the para-social which prevents the qualic exchange being hierarchically driven. It would be easy to assume that the uneven nature of para-sociality might result in an unfair weighting in favour of the performer. However, the para-social, and the resultant imaginative leaps it requires of the audience, allows space for a more heterarchical process of exchange. In some ways, the para-social and its unranked structure finds articulation through the language of Deleuze and Guattari. Within the para-social, the audience/performer exchange shifts towards a more rhizomatic structure. It opens up the possibility of a system of exchanges which map outwards, creating a more heterarchical, or centrifugal mode of transference. Of course, any invocation of Deleuze and Guattari is not without its own problems. It can be difficult for the reader of *A Thousand Plateaus*, who is usually engulfed by monolithic hierarchies, to engage in the rhizomatic process required for working through the book. One might call this process horizontal research, as opposed to vertical research which would require the reader to read through all the chapters from the introduction to the conclusion – culmination and termination points (Deleuze and Guattari, 1988: 22) – before the knowledge can be imparted. The difficulties that arise from *A Thousand Plateaus* could point to a failure in the rhizomatic process presented in a book format given that Deleuze and Guattari state that they

are writing this book as a rhizome. It is composed of plateaus. We have given it a circular form, but only for laughs. Each morning we would wake up, and each of us would ask himself what plateau he was going to tackle, writing five lines here, ten there [. . .] Each plateau can be read starting anywhere and can be related to any other plateau. (Deleuze and Guattari, 1988: 22)

In contrast, the para-social builds upon modes of engagement which are already familiar to the spectator; the sense of connection and exchange are already part and parcel of the daily intersubjective experience. As such, while the reader of *A Thousand Plateaus* might be required to 'unlearn' their normative relationship with the book, the audience experiencing the para-social need do no such thing. However, the success or failure of the rhizome-book is somewhat secondary within the context of our debate. Instead, we are invoking the rhizome as a way to point to pre-existing conceptualisations of difference and consider how a heterarchical approach to thinking about the moment of exchange in performance might serve us in our exploration of a shared affective state between audience and performer.

While not wishing to focus too heavily upon a methodological approach to knowledge creation, there remains something valuable in this approach which might yet help us to unpack that which we have termed 'the qualic exchange'. Through the folding of knowledge, Deleuze and Guattari offer understanding through affirmation and provide the reader with the knowledge without the object. The 'twofold' thought of Deleuze and Guattari is described by Stivale as a 'thinking shared by two' (1998: xi), an overlapping of two voices writing as one. Stivale adopts the term *'pensée à deux'* (1998: xi), to explain the system of knowledge employed by Deleuze and Guattari. In identifying the properties of twofold thought Stivale suggests a complication for the reader. Stivale recognises a form of slippage that occurs as an in-between which he terms 'intermezzo' (1998: xi), which is the gap between two sites of critical articulation.

It is through the *pensée à deux* that the potentiality of the intermezzo opens up. This thinking shared by two conceptualises the creative space that can be opened up between two equal parties. When exploring terminology that might capture the specifics of the intersubjective exchange between audience and performer, we were tempted to offer this as a development and shorthand for the terrain we are navigating. However, following discussion we came to recognise that the term doesn't quite fit the specifics of the audience/performer exchange. Although there are very clear analogues to the intermezzo, it is the potential held within para-sociality which marks out the qualic exchange as a different order of engagement. The intermezzo valorises the rhizomatic/ heterarchical approach and does so with parity at the heart of the understanding. We wish to strongly resist the opening of a false hierarchy within the performer/audience relationship and embrace the heterarchy of the para-social in which remains that which cannot be spoken between two subjective positions. It is from this un-knowing of one another that the transmission of affect occurs. Although there is an unevenness (although not inequality) to the qualic exchange, it does not offer a 'one-way' transmission. It allows the 'reality' of embodied processes to inform the experience for both participants. Within the qualic exchange, distance and uneven distribution of interpersonal experience is accounted for by the para-social, in which the appearance of connection encourages an experience analogous to Damasio's 'as-if' body loop, allowing for a connection which feels 'real' and thus functions as 'real'. If Heathfield calls for a recognition that there is no longer a clean distinction between absence and presence in performance, then we are positioning the qualic exchange as means to resist concerns regarding the real and the infelicitous in moments of affective transmission.

Tasks: Qualia

Alternative task for during the day:
Explore how small a performance can be in a train station* before it disappears.

Noticing an aspect
A concept developed by Ludwig Wittgenstein, Austrian-British philosopher.

Now I see a duck. Now I see a rabbit. I'm going to reference Wittgenstein now. I preface this in the way I am because I haven't really read that much of his work; read little and understood less. Perhaps that is why I am drawn to his duck/rabbit. We came across this simple line drawing in the final throes of writing up our PhD. It slotted into what we had been thinking with an elegance quite unlike anything else we had encountered. As we wrote about it, we became enthralled by the idea that once the rabbit had been seen, the duck is always infected by its presence, and (of course) vice versa. Once seen, it cannot be unseen.

Instructions
1. Place your micro and macro body/object in relation to/against the space of the train station*.
2. Explore the centripetal (draws towards the centre) and centrifugal (moves away from centre) body in the train station*.
3. Work solo to produce tiny performances to be performed at:
   12:00 p.m. for 15 minutes on Platform 1
   12:15 p.m. for 15 minutes on Platform 2
   and 12:30 p.m. for 15 minutes on Platform 3.

*Feel free to replace 'train station' with place of your choosing.

Tasks: Qualia

Dear Qualia . . .

> Make a list of instructions of How to Tell a Secret.
> Give it to a stranger.

> This is to be a solo act. Email me your thoughts.

Tasks: Qualia

Locate where you are.
Pay attention to how you sense and feel in this instant.

For me, this means getting into my body to locate any sense of uneasiness and to begin moving toward it to gain a greater understanding of **what is there**.

In order to help you with this, do the following:

I would like you to stand upright. I would like you to stand still and not move for 15 minutes. Arrive however you like and stay. Don't move.

Start to notice. Begin to increase your capacity to notice the details of how you bring yourself to stand still. Close or half-close your eyes. Move through your body with your attention and get a sense of **what is there**. Concentrate. Try to capture all the feelings and sensations throughout your body as you scan yourself head to toe and from the surface of your skin to the depths of your bones. Identify the difficult areas to locate. Focus on them.

Continue to work on finely discriminating between the different areas in your body and the arising sensations.

Continue noticing what you can until your time is up. Was that 15 minutes?

Next time, go through this process again.

And again.

Tasks: Qualia

Dear Qualia...
Deeds of hope

'Hope is not a lottery ticket you can sit on the sofa and clutch, feeling lucky. I say it because hope is an ax you break down doors with in an emergency; because hope should shove you out the door, because it will take everything you have to steer the future away from endless war, from the annihilation of the earth's treasures and the grinding down of the poor and marginal [...] To hope is to give yourself to the future, and that commitment to the future is what makes the present inhabitable'.

from *Hope in the Dark* by Rebecca Solnit (2004) pages 4–5.

Hi,
There is a beautiful tree – all covered in yellow right now. It is outside the back door of the library (where IT are located). If you are in the IT dept and look up, you see blue sky and bright yellow tree. Gorgeous.
Gillian

> **Task for Gillian**
> Lie on the ground under the beautiful yellow tree and look to the sky. Perform a rehearsed reading of the *Brief Encounter* script.

> **Alternative Task**
> Lie on the ground under a car to shelter from the rain. Take pictures of people's feet.

Tasks: Qualia

Dear Qualia...

Five instructions for group survival

1. When it all gets too much, rest your forehead against a cool wall or window and wait. Wait some more and resume.
2. When you tire of new faces, carry one another through the corridor space.
3. Try to place your hand in a stranger's, let them take you somewhere.
4. Hide under a table, chair or bench, this has the effect of making you disappear.
5. A group act to prevent hyperventilation:
   Take your first paper bag (numbered 1.) and poke eye holes into it. Place over head. Make a mouth hole. Take the second paper bag (numbered 2.) and breathe into it. Slowly, in and out, in and out. After some time, retreat. Slowly.

Tasks: Qualia

Start from the end, work backwards and don't look for patterns.

Clarity, stillness and four stories that might be true.

Tasks: Qualia

Dear Qualia...
I love to score ten out of ten

Things to do over the weekend

****

Write 100 tiny silent plays.

****

Make a temporary monument to something/someone you care about.

****

Track 'blue' across a city.

****

Repeat.
Repeat.
Repeat.

****

During rehearsal of *When We Dead Awaken*, Robert Wilson instructed the actors not 'to bounce dialog back and forth like a ping-pong ball. Let the words fly past each other. Don't pick up each others' rhythms. Follow your own line. Each of you is lost in a separate world' (Wilson, in Holmberg, 1996: 67).

So, follow your own line.

And at all times, remember:

When you are walking, stop and smile at a stranger.
Untitled (2002) by Louise Bourgeois

****

Repeat.
Repeat.
Repeat.
****

Tasks: Qualia

Dear Qualia...

> **'Tonight at 8:30'**
>
> Create individual performance interventions in the same place on a daily basis at the allotted time. This work should run for at least seven consecutive days and be documented..

Tasks: Qualia

Quiet zoning

Spend one week in silence together: you and your audience.

Tasks: Qualia

Quietly shouting

In the 'quiet carriage' on trains send performance instructions to your collaborator using CAPITAL LETTERS

Tasks: Qualia

Types of silence

David Lynch's films are full of different types of noisy silence. He creates and utilises them like a musical score. They have substance, a palpable quality.

Collect and document different types of silence.

Tasks: Qualia

How do you smell something?
Can you train yourself to perform through smell?

We've always sought out petrichor, that delicious odour that accompanies the first rain after a long period of warm and dry weather. You will find us running for the exit with nostrils aimed high.

Can you smell fear?
Place sanitary pads under your armpits and undertake a series of scary experiences:

Go on funfair rides: the louder your scream the faster you go.
Ask a friend to jump out from behind furniture to try to elicit a sense of fright.
Make a speech without notes or preparation to an audience of at least twenty-five people.

Place your fear-sodden pads in Tupperware and freeze. Take out to smell when you need to feel frightened in a performance.

Does the same smell experiment work for love?

Tasks: Qualia

We are convinced that there is such a thing as 'city noise', where a kind of generic sound emanates from the streets of cities.

However, we wonder if each and every city also has its own distinct soundscape, its very own particular aural environment. Please carry out this experience for us by travelling around the cities of the world, recording and describing the sounds that you hear.

Tasks: Qualia

Invent a machine dedicated to the collection of every intake of breath.

These inhalations can then be saved for a later date.

Tasks: Qualia

If the smell of freshly baked bread can filter through our nostrils as we enter the sliding doors of a supermarket, what artificial odour would be introduced at the beginning of your performance piece?

Create a smellscape

Create a performance that uses smells as its primary source. Explore generic and specific smells produced by actions.

How hard and fast do you have to run for your audience to smell your fresh sweat?

When you cook on stage does your audience drool in response?
Does your audience smell you before they can see you?

Tasks: Qualia

Stand in a fresh place. Stand where no one has stood before (snowfall can help with this task).

What do you do to mark that place?

Tasks: Qualia

The hour between the dog and the wolf

My favourite time of day has always been what some call 'the blue hour'. It speaks to the period of twilight each morning and evening where there is neither full daylight nor complete darkness.

So, here are some of the things that I have seen in the blue hour:

Floating lights in the corner of my eyes
A man pissing in a corner
The first one to decide to turn on their headlights
A button that catches the light and then is gone
A face that catches the light and then is gone
A running woman, sweating or crying
Not being able to distinguish between one stone and another
A bus tucked up for the night
A fire that is out of control
A fight that is out of control
A hand that is out of control
A heart that is out of control
Hair that is out of control
Skin that is out of control
Noise that is out of control
A skein of geese flying high overhead
Christmas shoppers
A scolded child
A swaying truck piled with bales of hay which throws stray bits in its wake
The sea coming in
A man watching the sea coming in
A couple in a car watching the sea coming in

Tasks: Qualia

A tree
Hotel architecture
Tarmac
Horizon
The logic of crowds
Val's Place
Sleepy travellers
The way a crutch hits the ground
The framing of the hills
A small act of kindness
A nod of recognition
A sleight of hand
A tearful goodbye
A tearful goodbye
A goodbye
Goodbye.

Once again, and only if the opportunity arises, ask, 'What's the light like here in [insert place name here]?'

> This time of day is also called 'the hour between the dog and the wolf'. Describe some of the things you have seen during this hour, and recreate in a performance space at the appropriate time.

Tasks: Qualia

Dear Qualia...
Helps

Today has been a little more eventful than I would have liked

Hold me

I'm trying to concentrate on my breathing

I'm working on dropping my shoulders, but they keep creeping up

Don't look at me

Really, stop

I know you don't mean to, but this is making me feel very self-conscious

It's just that I feel the weight of expectation in your stare

OK, look, if I sing you a song, will you leave me alone?

(bow)

Intersubjectivity and Affective Exchange

In some ways, this book started being written in the Bowen West Theatre in Bedford. It doesn't exist anymore, nor does the university that housed it. Actually, the building is still there, and it is still on a university campus, but both have changed their names. It was in this theatre, a theatre that is sort of no longer there, that I first saw Baktruppen. Like the venue which housed them, there is no longer a Baktruppen. Years after my first encounter with them, I saw them split up. Or rather I attended the most superb talk in which three of their number reflected upon the work they had made since 1986, the shifting constituency of the company and the fact that there didn't really seem to be enough of them to carry on working. They didn't formally split until a year later, but there was a palpable sadness to the proceedings, as if we were watching people deliver their own eulogy. I suppose that in a way we were. Watching them talk about their work, about their approach, about the fearlessness with which they approached making theatre was a humbling experience. And as they talked about the slow fading of the company, I felt the emotion begin to build; I started to find it difficult to swallow; and before long I was listening to strangers talk about some work I had seen, some work I hadn't, all the while tears ran down my cheeks.

This wasn't the first time that they had made me cry. That happened in that theatre in Bedford, the one that sort of doesn't exist anymore. I know that Bob has already written about the tears she experienced while watching *The Artist Is Present*, about how being on the receiving end of tears that weren't meant for her was a discomfiting position to find oneself in. I'm coming at tears from the other side, from the position of he who sheds them. The piece that prompted these tears was Baktruppen *Do&Undo* (2004), a piece that knots and unknots during three entrances, two exits and one turning point.

116

By the time we went to see them, Baktruppen was a company that had ghosted us for over a decade, from the first time we heard about a company taking sleeping pills and racing to see who could stay awake longest, the last man standing hitting a big red button which set off outdoor fireworks inside, to the point later when we first saw them live. Since then there have been various performances, videos, lectures and workshops, and ultimately the disbanding of the company. Despite our long history with them, we have never approached their work from any kind of critical perspective. This is possibly because of a specific moment within *Do&Undo* that has resisted critical engagement simply because of its power to unman us both. Whenever we talk about *Do&Undo*, revisiting our strange experience of this piece, we return directly to the moment that haunts us: the fulcrum point of the performance being the moment where a female performance member starts not just to cry, but to really cry, with sobbing and snot and shaking – she is inconsolable and still looking towards the audience. It was at this point that I experienced my own unravelling, where as an audience member the pleasures to be taken from understanding something dissipated, and I was only concerned with feeling something. I experienced a shift from watching them, to being with them. Perhaps my experience is best captured in the following observation:

Baktruppen is not perfect. Baktruppen is not good. Baktruppen is like you and me. And that is good enough. Everyone who is alive at this moment, is last. All the geniuses are old and dead. We are all Baktruppen'. (Andersson, 2009: 21)

It's not so much that I became Baktruppen through watching them, but that my relationship to them was not cognitive, but humoral. The tears brought me into the piece without the need for me to understand the meaning or the reason. Instead, I experienced a human-to-human moment in which I didn't know why it was happening, only that I felt what she did. The tears were shed in the middle of the first act, the 'Do' of the title. Perhaps it was this placing that caused the surprise, allowed me to feel the sucker punch of emotion. The piece began with the performers holding themselves in a human chain formation, and by lying on their backs they pulled and pushed one another along and across the front of the stage floor. The audience were treated to a deliberate and unapologetic exposure of bodies, where sweat stains marked the folds of their shiny unitards: skintight one-piece garments with long legs and long sleeves, stopping at the wrists and ankles, sheathing ageing bodies and offering no place to hide. Lars Ring in the Swedish newspaper *Svenska Dagbladet* described it thus:

> Imagine seven voluptuous Norwegians who are dragging themselves across the stage, while in different ways clinging to each other. Feet are squeaking against the floor, there are puffs and panting, and as a back ground there is the sound of a tired, notched version of the adagiettot from Mahler's 5th. The performers are dressed in tight body suits, and all the middle-aged defects – fat, grey hair, loose skin, fleshy sexual organs – are emphasised with merciless exposure. (in Andersson, 2009: 20–21)

This choreography was funny. The performers struggled, happily looking ridiculous, leaving little Rorschach blooms where they paused too long on the rubber dance floor. It was from this comical conga that she came forward, stepped towards the microphone and cried. Her sobs went on for minutes, and as her ragged breath still hung in the air, she made her way back to the chain. The shuffling started up again, and as the performers reached the other side of the stage, they formed a line and paused to observe their audience.

There is little doubt that the tour and detour (where they travel back across the stage in Act Two, again in the 'undoing' of the title) is difficult for its audience. Questions as to the meaning emerged somewhere in the doing but were long abandoned as a lost cause by the time the undoing had arrived. In the performance of *Do&Undo* we experienced, a good portion of the audience, perhaps a third, left during the first half, many sighing and grumbling in exasperation, perhaps struggling to reconcile themselves with the tension that arose out of the apparent refusal of the company to demonstrate recognisable skill, opening up questions of quality. And yet for us the indication of what we were seeing was writ in the title: firstly a reference to its structure and the repetition and reversibility, intentionally pushing perceptions in its audience. Secondly, the title refers to its 'knotty' attempt to hold the ensemble together through haptic means, and also looks to what might happen when an audience attempts to unravel its meanings.

But all of this is conceptual play, and it is not the thing I return to when I think of the piece, something I do often. Instead, I find myself returning time and again to the tears. To the shift, where everything else fell away and I was left watching a middle-aged woman sit on a stage and sob. She was surrounded by her contemporaries, her peers, perhaps her friends, but they made no move towards her. She sat, she wept. For minutes. And something in me shifted. I remember holding Bob's hand tightly, leaning forward, wanting to do something, but not sure what, acutely aware of the chairs hemming me in, of the irritation in the air and of my very real need to move towards her. Before me there played out a transformation: the piece moved from a post-modern joke to the witnessing of something . . . something what?? Not authentic, not real. Not really. But something else. Something in between what I thought I had gone to see and what I saw? No, not that either. Something, perhaps, that sat for a moment outside of discourse. Something that denied my thinking, and allowed only my feeling.

As I write this, I can feel a massive can of worms opening, but perhaps it is this that has left Baktruppen's work unexamined for over a decade. And maybe now, as I try to find the right way to frame this, I see it refracted through those tears shed by Abramović, the ones that have received so much attention but failed to move me because I could see only their hollowness, the sense of counterfeit and ultimately their absence. And I realise I am being unfair, unkind. In this moment, I lack generosity. So I stay with the realisation. Perhaps those tears weren't shed for Bob, but that doesn't make them any less real, any less felt. Now I have to reflect why the tears in Baktruppen, tears that were certainly not shed for me, had such an effect.

* * *

For me, Baktruppen isn't about crying; it's about laughing. Maybe that's because despite the arresting experience of watching *Do&Undo*, it's not really how I remember them. I like to remember the time I was at a football match with Baktruppen.

It wasn't really a football match. It was more like a football match that thought it was a performance. Or a performance that thought it was a football match.

I don't know what this performance was called; I don't even know if it had a name. I don't know if any of my recollections are real, but I do know that I hold them dearly. It feels appropriate, writing here about something I can't fully remember, something where the crisp edges have frayed and that runs the risk of being a 'soft touch' (Ahmed, 2014: 3), a memory so vague and steeped in unknowing. However, I am emboldened here by Knut Ove Arntzen and Camilla Eeg-Tverbakk in *Performance Art by Baktruppen First Part*, when they affirm in their editors' preface that '[s]urely, there are many more ways to experience and think of and with Baktruppen, stories that are yet to be told' (Arntzen and Eeg-Tverbakk, 2009: unpaginated).

My first encounter: I stood inside-outside in a room, doors flung open onto a wide stretch of concrete. The inside-outside room held a table and three microphones on stands. At each of these microphones there was a performer reading from the plays of August Strindberg and Henrik Ibsen. Sometimes there were bodies to speak the different parts of characters, but more often than not two of the microphones would stand abandoned, and the solo reader took on all parts, barely taking a breath between lines. The voice of the performers was broadcast across campus, bellowing out of massive speakers. Away from the microphones, there were other bodies, many other bodies. They were messy and chaotic, playing a very noisy football match on the concrete – the Ibsens marked by yellow strips of fabric tied around the waist, the head or the arms, and the Strindbergs similarly marked by green.

There was a table in the inside-outside room. The table seemed important; it was at least as significant as the football match. Upon closer inspection, I could see that it was in fact many tables, all pushed together to form a long line: it was a table for a banquet, a banquet that would last for the duration of the performance. People could go up to the table whenever they felt the need; performers, audience members, people from other parts of the campus drawn to the noise. Like placing food on a plate, where your potatoes become the mountains in the distance, these items on the table were similarly curated. At the back were bottles upon bottles of alcohol, all different colours. It looked as if everyone had raided the back of their parents' cocktail cabinets, looking for bottles, the dustier the better. There was jaundiced Advocaat, Campari blushing red at its bitterness and Midori of the brightest green. Towards the front of the table was a cornucopia of cupcakes and donuts and party-size bags of cheese and onion crisps, all hurriedly dumped in piles. Just looking at this table made my head hurt and my teeth sing.

During this ten-hour football-performance-match, a war waged between the Ibsens and the Strindbergs, celebrating the culmination of Baktruppen's intensive week of workshops at Dartington College of Arts in November 2007. This experience had seen the second-year theatre undergraduates making musical instruments out of turnips to feed the cows, an experiment to see if they could change the time of their lowing; they sang for hours in the rain and provoked the ire of security when caught en masse on the roof, searching for a different perspective. Robin Deacon discusses a parallel undergraduate university experience of Baktruppen's performance in *Performance Art by Baktruppen First Part*: 'The set is rubbish . . . old junk and office furniture disposed of and left to rot in the university car park. If you look very carefully, you can see the fireworks set within the stacks of broken swivel chairs and battered Formica desks. . . .' (Deacon 2009: 119).

At Dartington, the Strindbergs versus the Ibsens contained no fireworks, as least none that I saw during my repeated visits. This absence of pyrotechnics was something of a disappointment, but probably a state of affairs preferable to the campus security. In a lecture they gave the evening before the match, members of the company spoke of their piece *Spect* (1999), which concluded by letting off fireworks inside the Museum for Contemporary Art, Oslo. As I fell asleep that night, I hoped the dawn would bring a blaze of fireworks, their afterimage to be burnt into my retinas, but it wasn't to be the case. Instead, something else was seared into my vision: the laughing, sweating, exhausted faces of the second-year students, transfigured into something that surpassed the flash of coloured explosions; they became, however briefly, family. Two teams, yes, but a single unit intent on bringing out the best in one another, no cliques, no factions. When I close my eyes now, instead of seeing the after image of fireworks, I see the ghosts of these students, gently haunting all the subsequent students I have seen perform.

As I think of them now, I remember the concept of hauntology and the section in Jacques Derrida's *Spectres of Marx* in which he explores the hierarchy of each of Karl Marx's ten ghosts. He tells his reader that '[t]hey are labelled, a number is sewn on their backs as if they were playing on a soccer team the night of the big final beneath the lights, from Ghost No. 1 to Ghost No. 10' (Derrida, 1994: 174). As I think of them now, I wonder if Marx's ghosts make as much noise as mine. Sometimes, I fancy I can still hear their shouts, words not quite making sense as they nevertheless interrupt the Devon valley darkness. I cannot help but smile as I imagine the 'again walkers', locked in an eternal battle of two halves: Hedda tackles Arvid, the Count blocks a shot from Helene Alving, and the ref blows the whistle as takes Torvald a dive.

* * *

This, the final section of the book, is entitled 'Intersubjectivity and Affective Exchange', and serves as a means to more explicitly consider what is happening in those moments between the audience and the performer. Understandably, any consideration of such exchanges in live performance will be flawed. In most live performance practices, the performer will enact a series of behaviours, sometimes the representation of a fictional action, sometimes the execution of a task, and these enactments will often be performed multiple times in front of a variety of audiences. However 'expert' a viewer, there is an imbalance in experience, with the performer having had more time to understand and embody the moments of exchange. Despite the multiple actions that form the basis of the performer's experience, it is important to remember that one fundamental 'truth' remains: each iteration of a performance, however rehearsed, is being done for the first time. As a result, all experiences are freighted with a sense of the unique, something specific to this exchange in this moment. What happens when the edge of one subject position encounters the edge of another? The work of Baktruppen serves as our way in to this, but this will not be the only point of reference. Baktruppen, in both *Do&Undo* and in the extended football match, use the unexpected as a means to interrogate exchange in performance. The points of meeting, although significantly different, are central to an understanding of the work. *Do&Undo* uses the unskilled body to force the audience to consider their role; why should we be watching bodies no more adept than our own perform a piece of choreography? What makes this worthy of our time or attention? The football match between the Ibsens and Strindbergs asks similar questions about spectatorship, but in this instance the question is less 'Should we be looking?' and more 'Why am I not playing?', both challenging the normative interface between audience and performer.

In the 'Audience' section of this book, we suggested that when considering *The Artist Is Present,* Paco Blancas's body functions as the border from which the behaviours of the audience spring. His repeated visits, his appearance on blogs and tumblr pages, the increased visibility of his body and the re-performed cues it enacts helped to prescribe other moments of audiencing. We suggested that he became a boundary that held the performance in place and thus prescribed expected responses. But Blancas does more than unintentionally police the behaviours of other sitters, it does more than offer the museum guards a model of best spectatorial practice. Instead, we can see the borders offered by Blancas as a reminder of Martin Heidegger who observes:

> A boundary is not that at which something stops but, as the Greeks recognized, the boundary is that from which something begins its presencing. (Heidegger, 1971: 152–3)

The idea of a boundary, a line which marks the edge of a territory, is particularly useful when considering what happens in the space between an audience and a performance. Heidegger's assertion that a boundary is the point from which something emerges offers a different perspective to the more commonly understood sense that a boundary indicates the point at which something ends. In performance, and particularly at the point where the audience and the performer meet, it is more helpful to think of the presencing offered by Heidegger than of more formalised demarcation of behaviours that seek to keep the audience and performer in their separate spheres of influence. Perhaps Blancas was not offering a pattern of behaviour; perhaps the knowledge of his twenty-one sittings offered up permission to other spectators to meet the work in the way they needed to. Or more likely, his boundary was both a beginning and an end; an opening up of potential, and a fixing of expected behaviours.

From the start of the twentieth century, theatre practitioners such as Brecht and Brook have looked for ways to move the audience out of the dark of the auditorium, away from a presumed passivity and into more complicit relationships with live performance practice. Despite these numerous challenges, the predominant mode of engagement has been to keep the audience distanced, either through proxemic arrangement or a series of performance behaviours designed to reinforce the audience's invisibility. Although there have been challenges to the status quo that have encouraged audiences to become more integrated, such attempts retain a sense of novelty. Recent explorations of immersive performance, and the academic writing which has followed, have sought to point to the potential when audience and performer are no longer kept apart, the key idea being that it is at this point that 'something begins its presencing'. As considered in the previous section, although it is tempting to think in terms of an increasing democratisation, a number of academics have called this simple equation (visibility = engaged autonomy) into question. In his essay 'Politics in the Dark: Risk Perception, Affect and Emotion in Lundahl and Seitl's Rotating in a Room of Images', Adam Alston opens up questions about exchange when he asks, '[W]hat kind of politics takes place in dark theatre spaces?' (2013: 217). By analysing his experience of engaging with an immersive performance in which lights faded and the scenographic dimensions of the work were altered, Alston is able to reflect upon the manner in which the experience led to 'a submissive diminishment of control over [his] own behaviour' (Alston, 2013: 225). Despite the fact that Alston surrenders to the situation, inasmuch as he has chosen to be an audience member for *Rotating in a Room of Images*, he makes clear that many of his responses to the piece are autonomic, that is to say they are bodily responses, the by-products of a mechanism of survival evolved over millennia. The affective states evoked by darkness and disorientation were central to his experience of the work, as he observes that

> [l]ike the child fearing monsters under the bed at night, I was positioned by the performance in such a way that affective and emotional sources could be
> · called forth from the shadows, ultimately manifested in trips and stumbles through the space. (Alston, 2013: 223)

As Alston makes clear, although he is made a central part of the narrative experience, with the politics of projected agency allowing for the development of meaning, it would be hard to typify such an encounter as democratic – no matter how willingly the exchange is entered into. Responses are drawn from his body/mind as a direct result of environmental conditions.

As we made clear in the previous section, it is not our intention to position interactive experiences as spaces of 'democracy' per se, but nor do we wish to diminish them as potent contexts in which the space between the audience and the performer is being explicitly considered, as spaces in which the boundary is not an end, but the point from which the communication and perception of image, shape, form, structure, and narrative leads to shared understandings and affective states. In performance studies, the notion of the intersubjective exchange has become an ever-increasing area of debate, with that which passes between the maker of the work and the witness to said work being a focus of interest for the scholar. By shifting our attention away from work which relies upon or develops a specific type of audience/performer interaction (cf. Welton; Chatzichristodoulou and Zerihan; Machon; White; and Hill and Paris), or work which grows out of a particular reading strategy (cf. De Marinis and Schechner), this section hopes instead to explore the potentially messy hinterland where relationships and responses are less clear. We are not interested in making a case for modes of spectatorship being tied to specific genres and forms. As Bruce McConachie observes, 'Although some theorists and practitioners claim otherwise, conventional and immersive modes of spectating share the same foundations' (2013: 184), and it is these foundational elements that will be our focus. We are interested in exploring those exchanges that make up the experience of engaging with live performance practice. How exactly these moments of intersubjectivity might be understood and articulated without calling upon metaphor or relying upon a mythologising of the experience will be the main focus of what follows. As audience members, we 'know' that something is shared in the moment of exchange, that we are substantively changed by the simple experience of witnessing. But just what constitutes this exchange, and what is held in the pregnancy of the gaze? It is just this cognitive uncertainty, married to a 'gut feeling' that something just happened, which informs the two stories about Baktruppen at the beginning of this section, and why we want to return to them again before moving on.

We have this friend called Dani. She hasn't always been our friend; she used to be our student. The night we went to see Baktruppen was the night Dani almost crashed our car. Dani wasn't driving. Dani was in the back. Dani was apoplectic with rage. Perhaps we should offer a clarified version of this incident. The night we went to see Baktruppen was the night Dani almost caused our car to crash. That's better. It is a more accurate reflection of what happened. Dani didn't connect to the tears; she didn't find joy in the shambolic but sincere attempts to dance. She was furious. She said, if we hadn't been giving her a lift home, she would have left with all the others. Her response to the work differed wildly from the one described by Wesemann, who noted of one of Baktruppen's performances that

[a]fter fifty minutes no one in the audience gets up to leave. No one flees the theatre space. Everybody stays seated. A Performance is like a living room,

from which one does not have to be thrown out, as opposed to theatre, where the audience can only indicate what is to be indicated through their applause: obedient respect. (2009: 41)

In contrast, Dani's rage was so intense, so palpable, that she caused our small car (a 1l Ford KA) to fishtail across lanes on the M1. At first it was funny, but her railing against the world, her very real sense of the injustice that such terrible performance could get made became gradually more and more physically extreme. We pulled into a service station in order that she could stomp around in a more secure environment. We both offered her explanations, readings, a sense of what we could see that she couldn't. But none of these things worked. And nor should they. What we 'like' or 'hate' might be informed by what we understand, but that is not the sole motor of a response. There are things we understand that we don't enjoy, and things we don't understand that can transport us. This apparent confusion is echoed in the writing of Andersson, when he reflects upon his teaching of Baktruppen's work:

When I was lecturing on different aspects of contemporary theatre history at the Dramatic Institute in Stockholm, a student put his hand up and asked, 'I follow everything you say about Jan Fabre, Robert Wilson, Rimini Protokoll, Laurie Anderson and so on. But what is the thing with Baktruppen?' In my recollection of the situation the student cleared his throat and reformulated the question, 'Why do you like Baktruppen? I don't get it.' (It is nice to get a personal question.) Inside of me stories are bubbling up, some of them personal experiences, others, most of them, retold. But which one to choose? Do I have to convince the student? Straight away I end up in a discourse on quality: Baktruppen is not good, I say. Baktruppen is bad, really bad, undeniably so if you use established standards of quality within theatre. But, if you don't try to be good, are you in that case bad? (Andersson, 2009: 16)

Dani's response was no less affectively driven than our own, and no less framed by questions of quality than the responses of Andersson's students; it simply sat in a different register. Even across the divide of an auditorium, this company had provoked tears, laughter, and rage. What happened to provoke each of these individual and competing responses is central to what follows.

In the previous section, we touched briefly upon the role proxemics play in the performance of intimacy. Although this remains of clear value in understanding intersubjectivity in performance, we believe it is more than close physical proximity that engenders feelings of intimacy and affective exchange. That something happens in the exchange is a given, but we are interested in just what this might be. As a territory of enquiry, intersubjectivity has aroused interests in the cognitive sciences, social cognition, neuroscience, philosophy, psychology, psychoanalysis, and the social sciences. This list is not exhaustive, and as the term becomes of value to an ever-widening constituency, the meaning will continue to shift and expand. For the purposes of this writing, we draw on the definition offered in *The Shared Mind: Perspectives in Intersubjectivity* (Zlatev et al.), which states, 'In the simplest terms, intersubjectivity is understood [. . .] as the sharing of experiential content (e.g. feelings, perceptions, thoughts, and linguistic meanings) among a plurality of subjects' (Zlatev et al., 2008: 1). Intersubjectivity considers what passes between two (or more) subject positions, and offers up the mechanism by which the individual consciousness moves out of the solipsistic and into a more relational engagement with the world. In psychology, the term is often taken to mean those moments in which communication is non-verbal, allowing for a more body-centred understanding of interpersonal interactions to be explored.

Further, it is not just the exchange between two subject positions that is under consideration, but also the context in which such exchanges might occur:

> The body-subject responds to an environment. It is in dialogue with its environment and this dialogue is irreducible. Its actions can no more be understood without reference to 'its environment' than 'its environment' can be understood independently of the perception-action which gives that environment its nature [. . .] Subjects stand together in an I-Thou relation. Their actions interlock and engage, each motivated and coordinated by and through an orientation to the other, but without conscious positing and reflective awareness of either self or other. (Crossley, 1998: 32)

Here Crossley invokes the writings of Martin Buber to explain the relational nature of these exchanges, recognising the intersubjective as a complex series of relational engagements with one's own corporeal self, with the environment it occupies and through dialogue with other subjectivities. The intersubjective is a way to shift from the solipsistic to the relational, which has in turn been connected to a phenomenological engagement:

Husserl, the founder of phenomenology, has only recently been properly understood in the Anglo-Saxon world to be concerned not with the nature of private experience, but with structures of experience which give us a common life-world, serving as a pre-condition of any objectivity [. . .] Other scholars such as Merleau-Ponty (1962), Scheler (1954) and Schutz (1966) continued this tradition and developed complementary accounts of intersubjectivity (c.f. Zahavi, 2001) whose common theme is that the basic forms of understanding of others are not inferential, but rather direct. (Zlatev et al., 2008: 3)

This shift from the solipsistic into a recognition of the agency of the other party being witnessed is explored by Buber in his 1937 book *I and Thou*. In it, Buber posits an existential shift away from the subject/object position (which he refers to as 'I' and 'It'), where each position is separate from another, towards an attitude in which the other is not separate, or at least not explicitly or obviously discrete. Central to Buber's writing is the recognition of the value of the relational and a concomitant recognition of a dualistic approach to the self: that the self cannot be understood in isolation from that which it meets, and is thus always already a product of social construction. We would suggest that it is this recognition of one's own existence in relation to that of another that is at the heart of intersubjectivity. This doubling of the self, an action that occurs in order to allow the intersubjective to emerge, is offered in the opening sentences of his book:

To man the world is twofold, in accordance with his twofold attitude. The attitude of man is twofold, in accordance with the twofold nature of the primary words which he speaks. The primary words are not isolated words, but combined words. The one primary word is the combination I-It; wherein, without a change in the primary word, one of the words He and She can replace It. Hence the I of man is also twofold. For the I of the primary word I-Thou is a different I from that of the primary word I-It. (Buber, 1937: 3)

Significantly, Buber is offering a version of the self spoken into being, with language presenting a space of the multiple. Here 'I' is not a singular and abiding self; it is a site of interiority, but also an exterior projection. In this way, we might position the 'I-It' and 'I-Thou' as offering a heteroglossic understanding of the self. Bakhtin's heteroglossia (literally 'many-voiced') refers to a 'perception of language as ideologically saturated and stratified' (Morris, 1994: 15). Or, as Holquist articulates it, heteroglossia is 'a way of conceiving the world as made up of a roiling mass of languages, each of which has its own distinct formal markers' (1990: 69), allowing a simple either/or binary to be resisted. Gardiner summarises the concept thusly:

> For Bakhtin, then, language is unitary only 'in the abstract', only if it is viewed as a reified 'grammatical system of normative forms'. When language is examined in terms of its actual utilization in the social world, it becomes apparent that there exists an irreducible plurality of 'verbal-ideological and social belief systems'. (1992: 36)

Whether the twofold nature of 'man' is recognised as an acknowledgement of the divine or of the social construction of the self doesn't really matter here. What matters is that we are not singular, discrete entities. Rather, we are networked beings, constructed through a rhizomatic series of exchanges, relationships and influences. We are speaking here of the performative nature of the self. In performance studies the intersubjective can be applied to the modality of audience/performer transference. However, we would like to suggest that there are some issues that remain live in this application given the inherently uneven basis for audience/performer exchange. Couple this with the ever-diversifying ways in which performance material is presented and the manner in which performers meet their audiences, and increasingly the current articulation of intersubjective seems somewhat lacking for the complexity of the moment.

As indicated by our discussion of Bennett, MacKenzie, De Marinis and Schechner in the previous section, definitions and modalities of performance practice have been in flux throughout the twentieth and into the twenty-first centuries. Many scholarly works have been written in an attempt to if not define, then at least broaden and corral a variety of processes, with the intention of offering some kind of mobile and mutable taxonomy. This territory is well worn, and it is not our intention to revisit the conversation, but merely to point out that definitions remain open to debate, with more and more behaviours being brought under the auspices of performance. Given the complexity of the terrain, it should be no surprise that the concept of audience is equally uncertain, with a significant range of behaviours expected from this singular term. From passive acceptance to deeply involved co-activation, an audience can be called upon to perform a wide variety of functions and roles. Given this, it follows that what passes between in the performer/audience dynamic will be subject to a wide variety of distinctions. Thus, a simple acceptance and application of intersubjectivity presents some issues as a means to describe the specifics of performer/audience interaction, and some further consideration of the mechanics of the term are required.

Perhaps the most evident concern arising from intersubjectivity in performance practice are the hierarchies of power at play within the performer/audience dynamic, issues that we began to surface in the previous section. Certainly these differ considerably depending on the type of performance work, the venue, the geographic location of the venue, and so on. All these impact upon the potential for exchange, even in the more small-scale or intimate performance contexts. Developing from the questions around democracy and empowerment raised in the previous section, no matter the layout of the venue, nor the intended level of interaction, the performer/audience relationship cannot offer simple equality. For the most part, the relationship between the performer and the audience is para-social, with the audience member being in ownership of more knowledge of the performer than the performer has of the audience. Of course, there are the occasional exceptions to this, for example when you go to watch a friend or loved one perform, but even then, a direct parity is not achieved due to the proxemics, layout and acculturated behaviours in play. In what might be termed traditional performance practices, this inequality is doubtless because the audience outnumber the performers. That said, even in more immersive and interactive performance practices, the weight of the relationship favours the performer. Even when a piece is constructed in such a way to mitigate against it, culturally speaking, the power is held on one side of the intersubjective exchange, which complicates further what is happening in the gap between.

Thus, it becomes necessary to unpack what has heretofore been an accepted and un-interrogated process. For the most part the meeting between audience and performer tends to be transactional in some way, which further complicates the relationship. Audiences might have specific expectations of a performer, which if left unfulfilled can lead to disappointment. This further confuses the apparently hierarchical nature of the relationship. An audience can withhold its attention (and thus money) and close a performance down; the audience has the fiscal upper hand even if the performer has the greater cultural visibility. As such, there is a disconnect at the heart of the audience/performer relationship, one which complicates the intersubjective exchange. Although it is necessary to pause and consider the apparent complexities and inequalities at the heart of the intersubjective exchange between audience and performer, ultimately the question of inequality does little to separate intersubjectivity in performance from intersubjectivity in daily life. No exchange is entirely equal; no exchange is without certain levels of hollowness. Complexity is simply part of intersubjectivity.

Despite accepting the complexity of the intersubjective exchange, there remains value in exploring further just what might be occurring in the moment between. Traditionally, the intersubjective has been written about as a cognitive or a psychosocial process (see above), rather than an embodied one. Thus, we wish to explore what impact a more physical understanding of the intersubjective might have on an understanding of affective states. The affective turn is the shift away from what might be articulated as a purely conceptual engagement with the critical analysis of social and cultural texts. As ever, the attempt to offer a definition has the potential to limit and simplify responses, with the risk being that the shift casts other, more conceptually driven cognate or methodological approaches as inherently flawed. This simplified binary is not the intention of the affective turn, nor is it the intention of our exploration here. Instead, engaging with an affective response to performance material offers a deepening of the critical and analytical tools at our disposal, allowing access as it does to those feelings that we might have previously resisted for fear of being too inexact in our reading.

Before going too much further, it might be helpful to reflect on the term 'affect' and consider its meaning. An early definition of affect comes from Silvan Tomkins, whose work on affect theory suggests there are a series of biologically determined states, separate from, but connected to, emotion. For Tomkins affective states have clear edges, whereas emotional states are messier and more prone to bleeding across. When attempting to find a definition of affect, Brian Massumi turns to the originator of the term, Baruch Spinoza:

> The concept of affect that I find most useful is Spinoza's well-known definition. Very simply, he says that affect is 'the capacity to affect or be affected'.

This is deceptively simple. First, it is directly relational, because it places affect
in the space of relation: between an affecting and a being affected. It focuses
on the middle, directly on what happens between. More than that, it forbids
separating passivity from activity. (Massumi, 2015: 91)

Massumi observes that 'the formula 'to affect and be affected' is
also proto-political in the sense that it includes relation in the definition'; significantly, this means that '[t]o affect and to be affected
is to be open to the world, to be active in it and to be patient for its
return activity (Massumi, 2015: ix). This sense of affect requiring
one to be both in and of the world is important for us in that it con-
nects strongly to the intersubjective. As Massumi suggests, it might
seem a simple observation, but to experience affective states is to
be part of a community; it is to see oneself in relation to others.
And in this extension of the self lies the capacity to move beyond
the limits of our bodies and the solipsism that might imply. Massumi states, 'I use the concept of "affect" as a way of talking about
that margin of manoeuvrability, the "where we might be able to
go and what we might be able to do" in every present situation.
I guess "affect" is the word I use for "hope"' (Massumi, 2015: 3).

Of course, Massumi is at pains to stress that he is not offering a
definitive response. Indeed, relying on one theorisation of affect is
likely to result in accepting specific agenda, however unintentional
the inscription. As Ahmed notes:

For Massumi, if affects are pre-personal and non-intentional, emotions are
personal and intentional; if affects are unmediated and escape signification;
emotions are mediated and contained by signification. Feminist ears might
prick up at this point. A contrast between a mobile impersonal affect and a
contained personal emotion suggests that the affect/emotion distinction can
operate as a gendered distinction.6 It might even be that the very use of this
distinction performs the evacuation of certain styles of thought (we might
think of these as 'touchy feely' styles of thought, including feminist and queer
thought) from affect studies. (Ahmed, 2014: 207)

Any reading is subjective, a product of gendered, social and cultural construction. In this sense, analytical readings are no more
accurate for their ignorance of feelings. Thinkings are no more
objective or reliable; they are merely more normative and thus
defensible. Teresa Brennan, in the introduction to her book *The
Transmission of Affect* (2004) points towards this discrepancy in

how feelings, and specifically for the purposes of our writing, their potential exchange, have been – to some degree – ignored by theoretical writing:

> Is there anyone who has not, at least once, walked into a room and 'felt the atmosphere'? But if many have paused to wonder how they received this impression, and why it seemed both objective and certain, there is no record of their curiosity in the copious literature on group and crowd psychological and psychoanalytic writing that claims that one person can feel another's feelings. (Brennan, 2004: 1)

With a focus upon the experience of the clinician working in a psychotherapeutic context at the fore, Brennan's account nonetheless provides some excellent material for the student of performance. In relation to Hill and Paris's consideration of intimacy being impacted by proxemics (see Audience section), Brennan's writing begins to offer an exploration why this might be the case. Rather than simply accept the truism that affective states can be experienced and shared in the space between individuals, she attempts to offer some clarity as to why this might be the case.

For Brennan, there is little doubt that affect is a physiological process, one which is deeply bound into the biological structuring of our earliest development. She postulates that affective transmission can be experienced as early as the pre-implantation of a foetus. Her suggestion is that an affective exchange occurs 'at the moment of the blastocyst's implantation in the womb' (Brennan, 2004: 91), a process which occurs between day 5 and day 9 after conception. Obviously the case being made by Brennan is speculative, but her argument is that '[t]his is the only point at which the "mother's blood" is not filtered by the placenta' (Brennan, 2004: 91). At a humoral level, this is a moment of unmediated exchange in which both bodily systems are able to connect without an intermediary. As she goes on to argue, the importance of blood within the transmission of affect is key, which in turn is an upending of Neo-Darwinist thought. For the Neo-Darwinist the individual is a contained and determinate system, and although it can be influenced by outside factors, its affects are its own. As a closed system, transmission happens only at the genetic level. Brennan is not denying genetic transfer; rather, she opens the potential for other routes of cross-over to be considered and accepted:

The affects are not inherited, or not only inherited. They also flow from this one to that one, here and now, via olfaction and the circulation of the blood. The relatively new discipline of psychoneuroendocrinology shows us this much. (Brennan, 2004: 75)

If we begin to accept the idea that affect operates at a physical level, this shifts significantly the mysticising of those unexplained feelings that one experiences but struggles to articulate. One such example appears in the notes written by Marcel Duchamp during the 1930s and 1940s. Found posthumously in 1968, these notes outline his concept of the infra-thin, which he articulates thus:

> The warmth of a seat
> (which has just been left) is
> infra-thin.
> (Duchamp, 1983)

The mysticism to which we refer above is illustrated in Duchamp's assertion, which, although capable of being illustrated, cannot be defined. Duchamp illustrates the infra-thin as

[f]ire without smoke, warmth of a seat which has just been left, reflection from a mirror or glass, watered silk, iridescence, the people who go through (subway gates) at the very last moment, velvet trousers their whistling sound is an infra-thin separation signalled. (Duchamp, 1983: 45)

Duchamp is clear that the infra-thin is resistant to definition, and is happy to point to those exchanges which typify the experience. In contrast, Brennan seeks to consider just what is happening under the auspices of affect. Her resistance to simply laying claim to the concept, without offering some attempt to theorise how it might function in practice, helps in grounding that which might otherwise remain diffuse. Brennan negotiates this to some extent in her consideration of the disjunction between our flesh, the subjective experiencing of it and the subsequent attempt to bring this forth into language. As she explains in her chapter 'Interpreting the Flesh':

Throughout [the book], I have depended on a definition of feelings as sensations that have found a match in words. In part, this definition was based on the clinical belief that relief and energetic release comes with the words to say it. Language releases us from the affects (through genuine psychoanalysis or other practices of discernment) via words that express something occluded and thereby releases the energy deployed in this occlusion. The right words dislodge the misperceptions generated by the foundational fantasy. But words do not do this of themselves. They are pushed by the life drive, that is, the senses and the informational channels of the flesh that, I have argued, are intelligent, aware, and struggling either to subdue or communicate with a slower, thicker person who calls itself I. (Brennan, 2004: 140)

Within the context of poststructuralism, the idea of the 'right' words presents a whole range of concerns: that words might be anything other than culturally agreed upon markers liable to slippage and erasure, that words can contain 'truth', that words – already inscribed with hegemonic norms and conventions – might be able to speak to or for experiences of alterity, all these offer some potential resistance to Brennan's understanding. That being said, and while we as writers fully accept our own reliance on, indeed infection by, poststructuralist analytical responses, we recognise that Brennan is looking for ways to move beyond the reliance on words, however much the unreliability of their signification is accepted.

This approach to affect, to see it 'as a project to explore promising tools and techniques for non-dualistic thought and pedagogy' (Sedgwick, 2003: 1) is shared by Eve Kosofsky Sedgwick, whose book *Touching Feeling: Affect, Pedagogy, Performativity* (2003) considers how emotions impact upon the generation of knowledge and inform subsequent actions. She asks:

What does knowledge do – the pursuit of it, the having and exposing of it, the receiving again of knowledge of what one already knows? How, in short, is knowledge performative, and how best does one move among its causes and effects? (Sedgwick, 2003: 124)

The potential for the performativity evokes the writings of J. L Austin, questioning as it does the active nature of language. Sedgwick queries what knowledge does, positioning it as an active force rather than as something one is a passive recipient of. Just as the reader is generative in the meaning, the meaning is concomitantly generative in the selfhood of the reader. This idea of the performative, that we speak ourselves into being, has its roots in Austin's theory that words 'do' something, and his investigation into the relationship between performed utterances and the manner of their execution. As illustrated when placing a bet or reciting marriage vows, Austin believed the words were active in the execution of the act:

> In these examples it seems clear that to utter the sentence (in, of course, the appropriate circumstances) is not to describe my doing of what I should be said in so uttering to be doing or to state that I am doing it: it is to do it. (1963: 6)

Austin's explanation of the performative recognises that certain words have the power of doing. Sedgwick is borrowing this same position when she asks what knowledge does, and by inference suggesting that knowledge is in itself a doing. Performance and the performative share the definition of 'the act of carrying out.' However, whilst there is apparent common ground between performance and performativity, there is a significant schism. As Austin states:

> The term 'performative' will be used in a variety of cognate ways and constructions, much as the term 'imperative' is. The name is derived, of course, from 'perform', the usual verb with the noun 'action': it indicates that the issuing of the utterance is the performing of an action – it is not normally thought of as just saying something. (Austin, 1963: 6–7)

Culturally, 'performance' has become synonymous with pretence. In the opening chapter of *The Presentation of Self in Everyday Life* (1990 [1959]) (itself entitled 'Performance'), Erving Goffman posits the idea that the self is a performance, and whilst he writes about both 'sincere' and 'cynical' performance (1990: 28), he also foregrounds the 'discrepancy between appearance and actual activity' (1990: 53). He writes convincingly about the 'performer' doing one thing, yet believing another. This idea of pretence is even more evident in the more generally understood sense of performance and its application within the arts. In both Goffman's and Austin's construction, performance is the exact opposite of the performative. Performance is about re-presenting, about feigning (both in the 'everyday' sense of Goffman and the 'special' nature of theatre). Hamlet doesn't die when he is caught by Laertes' poison blade. Not only does the actor stand to receive his applause, but 'Hamlet' will be walking the same stage, engaged in the same series of actions on the following night. Of course, something is 'done' in the theatrical performance, but for Austin this doing, however convincing in the theatre, is 'in a peculiar way hollow or void if said by an actor on the stage' (Austin, 1963: 22). The words do not do anything when Hamlet says 'O, I die, Horatio' (*Hamlet*, Act V, Scene II). This type of performative utterance is described as 'parasitic' (Austin: 1963: 22), lacking its usual potency. The convention of watching a theatrical performance allows us to suspend our disbelief and pretend it is really happening when we know it is not, whereas Austin's 'performatives' are 'doings' in saying for real (i.e. they have consequences in culture).

Although not wishing to dismiss the potential for theatrical performance (see below), we are aligning ourselves here with Austin and Sedgwick's use of performative as relating to those 'speech acts' that engage in 'doing', rather than in the problematised 'performatives' of Derrida or Butler, which point towards an infelicity of all action. Derrida questions the existence of the 'genuine' speech act of Austin, by positing that '"everyday language" is not innocent or neutral' (Derrida, 2002: 19), thus stating that all speech acts are 'infelicitous' in an Austinian sense. Already Austin has invoked the insincere in performance, and here Derrida similarly calls into question the sincerity of the performative. These conjoined ideas of sincerity or cynicism are interesting here not specifically in and of themselves, but rather in what they might afford in relation to a consideration of intersubjectivity and shared affect. The idea of the 'parasitic' opens up concerns and questions when thinking about the emotional landscape of performance. Once we move beyond catharsis, and the idea that the emotional charge building throughout a performance can be safely expended by the climax of the piece, the accusation of a parasitic landscape requires us to question if the implication is that performed emotions are somehow ersatz. When writing of the perceived threat to the United States from Saddam Hussein, Brian Massumi observes:

> It will have been real because it was felt to be real. Whether the danger was existent or not, the menace was felt in the form of fear. What is not actually real can be felt into being. Threat does have an actual mode of existence: fear, as foreshadowing. Threat has an impending reality in the present. This actual reality is affective. (Massumi, 2010: 54)

It is this palpable sense of anxiety emerging from 'fictional' or imagined experiences that Alston experienced in his spectatorship of *Rotating in a Room of Images*. Massumi goes on to offer the following proposition: '[I]f we feel a threat, there was a threat. Threat is affectively self-causing' (Massumi, 2010: 54). For Massumi, affect is real if felt, whether or not the event which led to the experience has a basis in objective reality. Thus, unlike Derrida's performative, affect is always trading in the real. In this way, conversations regarding sincerity or insincerity are rendered moot; affect is 'real' by virtue of it being felt. There is no objective exteriority to which it must conform in order to be rendered real; it is. Another way of exploring this is through the body loop of Antonio Damasio, or more specifically the 'as-if' body loop. Margaret Wetherell offers an overview of Damasio's ideas in her book *Affect and Emotion: A New Social Science Understanding*, in which she observes:

> Damasio's central argument is that the process of emoting takes place through what he calls a 'body loop'. Emotions travel through the brain and the body. The registering of this physical flow and the loop back as these changes are recorded and picked up by the brain becomes the affective experience. [. . .] Damasio insists that the body, including the brain, is 'the theatre' where emotions are performed and like [William] James, he insists that the body (in the form of neural activity in the brain and activity driven by the autonomic nervous system) precedes the feeling. (Wetherell, 2012: 34–5)

Interestingly, Wetherell picks up on Damasio's application of the theatrical metaphor as a way to conceptualise the body and brain as a site of agency. Unlike the theatre of Austin, in which the execution of an action is somehow rendered false, Damasio and Wetherell position theatre as a site of action without being overly concerned with the veracity of said action. Wetherell observes that Damasio's perspective 'allows for the possibility that cognitive events such as memories or other feelings might be the inducer' of an emotional state (Wetherell, 2012: 35). Wetherell expands:

> It is not just a simple process of external stimulus – body response – feeling. James' famous example suggested a sequence such as presence of a bear – running away – observation of self running away – feeling of fear. For Damasio, the sequence could well be cognitive event – body response – feeling instead. (Wetherell, 2012: 35)

It's not often I find myself wondering if this is joy. Wondering if the feeling that is welling up inside of me is an outpouring of goodwill to all of humanity. Sitting with the sensations that make my chest swell, my throat tighten, and my eyes sting. But in a good way.

This is not to say that I don't experience joy often. I do. Sometimes, I just find myself running. Not going for a run, not making the choice to get out my trainers and find some shorts, but just running. No concern for my footwear, my clothes, or even my destination. Just running because I suddenly feel so privileged to have arms and legs, and being taken by the urge to use them. This process usually makes me laugh; partly at the sensation, partly because I can see how ridiculous I must look from the outside. Running. Laughing. Not worrying about where I'm heading or who can see me. These outbursts don't last long. Too soon I find that I'm all sweaty, or I remember that, actually, I do need to be somewhere. But these moments exist. They erupt. I experience them, but I don't question them.

But sitting in the Richard Howard Theatre in The Place, London, I found myself thinking 'Is this joy?' It wasn't a thought I could stay with for long, as the audience was standing up, and we were beginning to file out. And as I did that strange sideways walk in between the seats, slowly heading towards the aisle and then the door, I realised I was not asking myself, 'Was this good/was this bad?' I wasn't engaged in a critical or analytical debate with the work I had just seen; I was absolutely in my own subjective experience, listening in to my body and reflecting upon what I was feeling, trying to find analogues not with other pieces of performance I have experienced, but trying to connect the feeling in my chest to other such feelings I have had in the 'real world'.

It is at this point that the 'as-if' body loop enters. Wetherell explains the process functioning as 'a form of internal stimulation rather than the stimulation [coming] from actual physical changes (Wetherell, 2012: 35). In this way, we begin to see a relationship between Massumi's conceptualisation of the reality of affective states and those expounded by Damasio. It is at the point of introducing the 'as-if' body loop that Wetherell draws parallels between Damasio's ideas and recent consideration of mirror neurons, which 'although contested [. . .] have been seen as evidence of the neurobiological bases of human inter-subjectivity and empathy' (Wetherell, 2012: 35).

Rather than opening out the term to further debate here, we wish to keep the connection between the performative and affect as surfaced by Sedgwick:

I would remark, though, on how both Derrida's and Butler's performativities, because they are in the service of an antiessentialist epistemological motive, can seem to be cast in the reverse image of the hypostatized grammatical taxonomies that have characterised, for example, John Searle's or Emil Benveniste's positivistic uses of Austin. (Sedgwick, 2003: 6)

I wish that I hadn't allowed that train of thought to proliferate. I wish I hadn't stood up. I wish that I had stayed in my seat, pulling my knees in towards my chest as other people were forced to do the sideways walk past me. I wish that I had sat there for a little longer, not trying to characterise the feelings I had, but just letting them be. But wishing for such a thing won't make it so, and all too soon the moment had passed. It was that interruption of the 'real world' that did for me. As soon as I wondered if this feeling of joy was the same one I felt in the 'real world', all sorts of critical and evaluative questions crowded in; what was unreal about this situation?

The piece seemed to have started before I had reached my seat. I thought that this felt a little odd, as I hadn't been dawdling outside, but already there was a conversation in full swing. There was a woman standing downstage left behind a microphone. She was quite small and spoke with an accent. I couldn't place it, but in fairness, I wasn't trying that hard. She seemed to be talking to some people on the front row, but I couldn't be sure. And on reflection, I wasn't really paying that much attention. I checked that I wasn't missing anything important (I didn't think I was), and I continued to make my way towards my seat. This was a Friday, the last night of a three-day trip to London with a group of students. This might be an awful thing to admit, but sometimes going to see performance feels like, well, like work. Pieces are chosen because of what they might offer the students, not because of what they might offer me. This is wholly appropriate, and not something that I am bemoaning; rather, I offer this as context. I'm not complaining (and if I were, I'm sure that I would need to hashtag 'middleclassproblems'). So what if I don't always want to go to the theatre. Who cares if sometimes I'm just a body to make up numbers, there to satisfy my university's health and safety policy?

As I made my way towards my seat, I had the vague memory of having chosen the piece. I remember looking at that the blurb on the website and thinking that it looked like it would be a good match for a mixed group of dance and theatre students. As I watched the woman mumble her direct address from behind the microphone, haltingly reading out other people's ideas of happiness from a clipboard, I figured that I was broadly right. She was talking. That's often a good sign in a dance house.

Clearly, the term 'performative' has become a multi-accentuated sign, resisting a fixity of signification, and has developed further to describe the 'nonessentialized constructions of marginalized identities' (Dolan, 1993: 419). Sedgwick's return to the Austinian performative is in part due to her use of Paul Ricouer's 'hermeneutics of suspicion' as a response to the particular types of reading strategies developed through poststructuralist approaches to textual analysis:

> [T]he 'hermeneutics of suspicion' [. . .] may have had an unintentionally stultifying side effect: they may have made it less rather than more possible to unpack the local, contingent relations between any given piece of knowledge and its narrative/epistemological entailments for the seeker, knower or teller. (Sedgwick, 2003: 124)

Offering his response to the ideas of Marx, Nietzsche and Freud, Ricouer's take is that these theorists offer an excessively suspicious view of ideological, philosophical and political dogma, suggesting their readings mask a fundamental paranoia. In her development of the idea, Sedgwick notes that '[i]n a world where no one need be delusional to find evidence of systemic oppression, to theorize anything but a paranoid critical stance has come to seem naïve, pious, or complaisant' (Sedgwick, 2003: 126), and she accepts a certain functional value to the concept. That said, despite Sedgwick's evident valuing of a suspicious approach to analysis, she is hesitant to accept this as the dominant mode of reading. Through an analysis of Ricoeur's concept, Sedgwick considers how poststructuralist criticism has assumed that this one (wholly appropriate and valued) approach is the default stance to take when approaching a text. As she develops the idea, she reflects that 'the methodological centrality of suspicion to current critical practice has involved a concomitant privileging of the concept of paranoia' (Sedgwick, 2003: 125), and it is this realisation that takes her to the teachings of psychologist Melanie Klein. It is by drawing upon these that Sedgwick offers a resistance to the paranoid/schizoid and instead embraces a depressive position. In the context of critical analysis, it is probably necessary to unpack some of this terminology and move it beyond the immediate psychoanalytic context that it implies. It is from Klein's observations on early childhood development that the paranoid/schizoid state emerges. In terms of psychoanalytic practice, this is a significant and necessary part of a child's development and continues to be a valuable part of an individual's psyche into adult life. As such, Klein does not offer the position as negative, and similarly Sedgwick is not calling for a complete cessation of the 'hermeneutics of suspicion'. According to Klein, the depressive position leads sequentially from the paranoid/schizoid position in a child's development. Similarly valuable in terms of the developmental process, the depressive position brings together the previously separated good/bad objects of the paranoid/schizoid into a union which allows the child to move towards a more empathetic engagement with the world. It is this shift from the paranoid/schizoid towards the depressive which leads towards an urge to repair. It is precisely this reparative process that Sedgwick positions as being central to the affective turn. Her aim is to offer a 'reparative criticism' which allows for '[t]he flexible to-and-fro movement implicit in Kleinian positions' to inform approaches to text which will see critical analysis functioning 'not as theoretical ideologies [. . .], but as changing and heterogeneous relational stances' (Sedgwick, 2003: 128). In this sense, the approach becomes more robust and allows for Sedgwick to address the function of knowledge. The question of what knowledge might do has an implied coda that might be worth articulating: what does knowledge do to us? Perhaps more specifically, what do the methodologies we use to unpack an experience do to the experiencing? To suggest that knowledge might affect those active in its pursuit is self-evident, but perhaps less immediately evident is that the manner in which the knowledge is pursued might also have an impact. It is this premise that leads Sedgwick to offer an alternative to the hermeneutics of suspicion. Indeed, she suggests:

> 'Criticism' may also not be the best way to describe reparative reading. Appreciation might come closer, not because depressive readers necessarily endorse textual agendas naively or exclusively but because of the way in which we might try to empathise with and articulate why a text adopted its specific strategies, recognising that it had done the best that it could. (Sedgwick, 2003: 12)

Her delivery was a little stilted, a little fumbling. She was trying to make connections to the audience, but the house lights were on, and people were still drifting in, engaged in the conversations we had started in the bar, in the foyer, on the tube. As an audience, we hadn't really arrived, and as a performer she wasn't doing enough to make us land. Watching her from my seat, I figured that this was just inexperience, and that it would give me something useful to talk to the students about later. If I knew that in little over an hour I'd be asking myself if the joy I was feeling was real, I might have been a little less dismissive. I might have paid a little more attention.

That's the thing about being in an audience. Even when you are packed in tight rows, plunged into darkness, and expected to direct your gaze towards the stage, no one can force you to engage. As a result, there tends to be a certain amount of coercion taking place, tricks and strategies to catch your eye. There are many ways to prompt the audience to engage; dim the houselights, open with a loud sound cue, have a performer 'make an entrance'. If you're reading this book, you have probably witnessed many such strategies, and maybe employed some of your own. When the audience is rendered a singular mass, the work needs to connect immediately, to draw everyone together, in order that a sense of community responsibility can develop. That way, we police ourselves, we shush the noisy, tut disapprovingly at the sweet rustlers, and glare at the coughers. It's about creating space in which tacit agreement of behaviours can develop in order that we all know what our roles are.

And this is precisely what Robert Clark's *Promises of Happiness* did not do. The houselights stayed up longer than I was expecting. There was no censure as I watched conversations continue in the audience, and there was no explosive opening; instead, there was just a slow unfurling of the work, a sense that we were being gently courted, encouraged to find our way in rather than coerced. The more I watched, the more I became certain that this was a deliberate strategy. Rather than force me to engage, I was gently encouraged to find my way towards the work and the four performers on the stage.

If a text can be let off the hook and be valued for having at least tried, so too should the bodies which fail and falter in the audience/performer relationship. To return to Brennan's position that the intersubjective exchange is physiologically grounded, it is helpful to consider how the body might function in the development of the intersubjective, in much the same way that Alston positions the importance of the autonomic in achieving affective states in immersive performance. As with the emergence of an interest in mirror neurons, recently much has been made about the presence of neurons in the structure of the heart and gut. Neurons are those cells that transmit electrical impulses along their pathways and are the central structuring cell of the nervous system. It has been discovered that the heart contains about 40,000 of these cells, leading to a great many web pages celebrating the 'fact' that our heart can 'think'. In the context of the 100 billion neurons that are contained within the human brain, to leap to an assertion that the heart has a cognitive process is possibly something of a stretch. That being said, the presence of neurons in areas outside the brain has not been dismissed without interest. In his paper entitled 'Gut Feelings: The Emerging Biology of Gut–brain Communication', Emeran A. Mayer observes that a

> major scientific breakthrough in understanding the interaction of the nervous system with the digestive system occurred with the discovery of the so-called enteric nervous system (ENS) in the middle of the nineteenth century. Even though it is now considered the third branch of the autonomic nervous system, the ENS has been referred to as the 'second brain', based on its size, complexity and similarity — in neurotransmitters and signalling molecules — with the brain. (Mayer, 2011: 1)

There is something about sharing an experience in the light, over sharing an experience in the dark. When the lights are dimmed in the auditorium, you can be anonymous, faceless. Obviously the people in the direct vicinity will be aware of your behaviours, but assuming that you do not act in a manner too outlandish or disruptive, it is unlikely you will draw more than a passing glance. Not so when the house lights are up. Then we are complicit; maybe not complicit in the way an audience in interactive work is, but complicit in our very audience-ness. When the lights are up, maybe you are supposed to have a better time, or at the very least let everyone know what a good time you are having.

As I settle into the environment, get used to the lights being up, I remember that Bob has been reading a book called *The Promise of Happiness*. It's by Sara Ahmed, and I wonder if it has anything to with the piece I'm watching. I don't think it does. As the piece continues, we are offered hugs, money, shots, cups of tea, and we are encouraged to close our eyes and think of someone special to us. I was already thinking of Bob and the book she was reading, but now I was thinking of her again. We are encouraged to phone the person we were thinking of, and we listen to the phone calls the four performers have made to those who are special to them.

Written down, it doesn't sound like much. And I know that words are failing me. They failed in the immediate aftermath, and they continue to do so months later. I only know that as the piece ended, with charm and wit, I was left with an overwhelming and elegiac sense of joy and wonder. On the way out, I tried to articulate something about the hesitance of the performer at the start, how she had wrong-footed us with this simple performance strategy, that Clark had found a way to unsettle the normative structuring of dance work. I tried to tell my colleagues that all this was part of the plan, that they didn't want us to know when the piece started, that they wanted a slow bleed into the piece, to keep us relaxed. At least, that's what I think I tried to say to them. But I kept laughing. I suspect that my colleagues, Victor and Prarthana, thought that I might be getting a bit carried away, that perhaps my critical facilities were a little dulled by the radical shifts in affective states I experienced throughout the course of this modest piece. And they might have been right. But my cheeks were hurting, and I wanted to run.

These 100 million neurons are considerably more significant in number than the 40,000 in the heart, but both give weight to the folk wisdom of listening to our heart, or trusting our gut, and the presence of nerve-cells, capable of transmitting information along their processes, gives weight to having a 'gut feeling', or being 'heartsick'. Mayer goes on to observe:

The first comprehensive scientific theory of brain–viscera interactions was formulated in the 1880s by William James and Carl Lange and was based on the central concept that stimuli that induce emotions such as fear, anger or love initially induce changes in visceral function through autonomic nervous system output, and that the afferent feedback of these peripheral changes to the brain is essential in the generation of specific emotional feelings. According to this theory, we feel anxious because we perceive our heart beating faster, because we become aware of our respiration becoming more frequent and shallower, or because we feel 'butterflies' in our stomach. In the late 1920s, Walter Cannon challenged the James–Lange theory, postulating that emotional feelings are generated directly by subcortical brain regions rather than from the feedback of situational bodily changes. He proposed that such bodily changes that are associated with emotional states are simply by-products of these brain changes, and that the visceral responses are too slow to play any part in the subjective experience of emotional feelings. (2011: 23)

This shift in understanding, from the theory offered by James and Lange positions the gut as a receiving device from the autonomic nervous system, to a process capable of generating information, opens up the landscape of embodiment, allowing the whole body to play its part in cognition. As Mayer further observes:

Damasio eloquently proposed that somatic markers (for example, memories of body states associated with previous feeling states) arise from positive or negative emotional feeling states being associated with visceral and other bodily responses (body loops) to certain contextual situations. According to this theory, these body loops, or their meta-representations in the orbito-frontal cortex (OFC), may play a part not only in how somebody feels at a given moment but may also influence future planning and intuitive decision making. (2011: 23)

The presence of neurons in the gut and in the heart thus gives some further credence to rejecting what Damasio has referred to as 'Descartes error' in his book of the same name and takes us further towards Massumi and Damasio's sense that feeling makes real the linguistically driven critiques of reality offered by both Austin and Derrida (although both come from significantly distinct positions) and might well be rendered somewhat moot in a conversation aimed at intersubjectivity and affective exchange. The body loop of the audience could thus be positioned as a form of training in which we become better at bearing witness simply through the performative, and its potential to be a doing in saying might thus be repositioned as a feeling in witnessing; that the experience might spring from the fictional does nothing to remove the potential for affect.

When Brennan speaks of the 'right' words, she is not positioning them as universal; rather, they are merely the key to unlock the affective. Significantly, Brennan positions language not as an absolute, but as a evolutionary error:

[T]here is the disjunction between the endless, infinite structure of the signifying chain and the finite concerns of neurotic subjects who are worried about birth and death and their meaning in the scheme of things. But there is an alternative explanation, other than linguistic mysteries, for this disjunction. The alternative is the notion that something went wrong in the scheme of things, something that split the order of signification from the orders of the flesh. The orders of the flesh, in this scenario, have become mortal, whereas those of signification remained infinite. The orders of the flesh, in this scenario, have become mortal because they are obstructed by something that slows them down. (Brennan, 2004: 147)

The slowing down of the flesh, and its rendering mortal through the intercession of lexical and linguistic means – to accept this dances us close to the edge of a Cartesian error, where the body and mind (in this case signified through language) are bifurcated. But perhaps this isn't an error at all, merely Brennan's way of reminding us that we have inherited two modes of understanding, two modes which we struggle to reconcile.

It is tempting to accept the evolutionary error of language and position it as a failure of sorts, a failure in coherence which has allowed an explicatory gap to open, a gap into which experience can fall. Certainly the idea of a disjunction between affect and cognition is nothing new, but how does this line of enquiry serve a deeper understanding of the transmission of feeling between subjects? In the next section we explore the idea of qualia, a way on which the explicatory gap of experience has been conceptualised. For now, though, we would like to return to an extended consideration of practice as a means to consider the transmission of feelings between subject positions. Tears were our way in to this section, so perhaps tears can be the way in which we find a conclusion of sorts.

In the opening section of the book, we touched briefly upon Plato's critique of poetry and the impact that had on the conceptualisation of the audience. Aristotle's counter to Plato's critique was through the recognition of catharsis as an engaged and engaging activity for the audience. For Aristotle, catharsis removed the suspicion of inactivity and passivity, positioning the audience as an active force within the drama. Questions of catharsis have surfaced and resurfaced throughout subsequent histories of performance analysis, from the critique offered by Brecht, through catharsis being offered as a defence for violent video games. Although we do not wish to dwell on these debates, it is helpful to touch on catharsis and remind ourselves that it has been a way to argue for activity in spectatorship for millennia. Catharsis has been used as a means to understand action and change, not just in relation to cultural product but also in psychoanalytic (Freud) and social (Durkheim) theory.

We mention catharsis here because there is the tendency to understand it through cognition. In his book *The Persistence of Romanticism*, Richard Eldridge asks the question:

> Is the catharsis of an emotion a matter centrally of its elimination or purgation from the body, here from the audience who has felt it, or a matter centrally of its ritualistic expression and discharge within the plot itself? (Eldridge, 2001: 147)

Essentially this positions the debate around catharsis as one of affect versus cognition. Is the importance of catharsis what it can do for the audience or what it can do for the audience's understanding of the plot? There are two pieces we would like to consider as a means to draw this section to a close, both by the Danish filmmaker Jesper Just, and both allow for a consideration of catharsis and plotting. For Just, narrative plays a lesser role than mise en scène in the construction of his work. As such, it is difficult to decide if the affective shifts afforded by his films are an example of catharsis or some other means to engender affect. Certainly, the absence of the live performer removes the direct psychoneuroendocrinologic, but the spectators' location in a gallery might afford a person-to-person affective exchange between them.

We first encountered *No Man Is an Island II* and *Bliss and Heaven* in 2006 at Kiasma, a museum of contemporary art located in Helsinki, Finland. Kiasma is Finnish for 'chiasma', which is an anatomical term for the crossing or intersection of two tracts within the body, for example when nerves or ligaments meet, and a meeting point is exactly how the work of Just operates for us – a place in which the affective and the cognate come together. In the first film, *No Man Is an Island II* (2004), Just presents a dark bar or nightclub containing five seated men, two sat together at a table, a further two sitting at separate tables and the last seated alone at the bar. None of these men look at one another. Each man wears a suit and tie, except for the youngest played by Johannes Lilleøre, who is dressed in a tracksuit top and jeans. This is a space populated only by men; there are no women in this world save for the flat representations of classical nudes painted on the wall behind Lilleøre and the topless cowgirl in the photograph behind the bar.

As with the later *Bliss and Heaven*, there is the sense that Just is gently revealing what might be happening behind closed doors. The camera pans across the bar, taking in all of the occupants of the space, until it settles on Lilleøre as he stands and begins to sing an unaccompanied version of Roy Orbison's 'Crying'. There are small reactions from the other men in the bar, none of them particularly positive, which makes their eventual engagement all the more surprising. At first it is the solo cigar-smoking man who joins in with a tenor accompaniment, followed by the two men seated together, until eventually the big man at the bar stands up to join in. The song is completed without any sense of engagement from the men, and the final shot sees tears coursing down Lilleøre's cheeks. In *Bliss & Heaven* (2005), the second of the two films we saw, one man (also played by Johannes Lilleøre) walks across a rural landscape until he encounters a lorry parking. He crouches down in the long grass and watches as the lorry driver gets out of the cab, makes his way to the back of the truck, opens the door and climbs inside. After a moment's hesitation, Lilleøre gets up and follows him in. As he makes his way through the interior of the truck, he finds the space opening up, and it reveals itself to be a large proscenium-arch theatre, and on the stage the truck driver soon performs without realising that he is being observed.

As with any description, the pieces themselves amount to considerably more than can be articulated here, and perhaps it is what cannot be written that reduced both of us to tears. Quite soon into the first viewing of *No Man Is an Island II*, we found ourselves holding hands and quietly sobbing. Curiously, this response didn't abate for the next film and the three subsequent viewings we sat through. We watched both films loop, and with each repeated viewing, the tears continued. Afterwards, we left the darkened gallery space and made our way to the café, both wanting the space to reflect on what had affected us so deeply. The minutiae of our conversation is not important here; we bring it up only to mention that we both felt strongly that the space would allow us to cry. We agreed that there was something happening in the gallery, something in the quality of silence that echoed the physical distance between the men in the films, a distance that was nonetheless profoundly supportive and accepting.

What we found surprising was the manner in which both pieces prompted an affective state without relying on the usual tropes of narrative and character, something which was able to 'speak' directly in a way that sidestepped the cognate or the analytical. This is not to dismiss the rich territory of analysis available when considering the work of Just; the conjoined concepts of bodies, spatiality, absence and presence emerge as significant areas for consideration. As a film-maker he is able to rely on the extension of time through the process of editing, and although the spaces in between his bodies are not the same as in live work, there remains an opportunity to consider the importance played by disappearance. Central to the responses to Just's work seems to be a positioning of his practice as exploring filmic representations and critiques of reality. Adam Budak observes that

> [i]n his video work Danish artist Jesper Just constructs an oneiric space out of a fragile tissue of primal fantasies and socio-cultural subjectivity [. . .] Just performs a masquerade of masculinity immersed in a frenzy of carnivalesque and uncanny séance. (Budak, 2005: unpaginated)

By evoking the twinned concepts of carnival and the uncanny, Budak offers up Bakhtin, Freud and Lacan as potential theoretical filters through which to read the work of Just. Indeed, by referencing the uncanny (however unintentionally), Budak also allows the reader to consider the attendant theory of abjection and thus wonder if Kristeva might fit in to his potential responses to Just's work. These are doubtless complex and interrelated territories that might serve as one way to conceptualise the ideas offered up by Just's practice. Certainly the idea of carnival and the Bakhtinian overturning of what is socially accepted and expected is fully evident in *No Man Is an Island II*. These are not men who are supposed to come together in harmony, any more than the bar should be considered as a venue appropriate for such a sharing. Culturally speaking, the expectation is that any coming together would be done through the excessive use of alcohol and barely contained violence. Instead, we are presented with a song about weakness, a song that offers a clear resistance to the expected modalities of the masculine, resulting in the significant queering of the landscape. As we do not intend to position affect as prelinguistic , it is inevitable that our analytical readings will inform our affective response; the gut, heart and head working together.

Perhaps as we sat in the dark of the gallery, what we were responding to wasn't just the turning upside down of expected behaviours but also the dreamlike status of the work suggested by Budak in his invocation of Bachelard. By offering that Just's work creates an 'oneiric space', we are reminded that these are not realist texts, and nor should they be responded to as if they are. There are no 'characters', no motivations, little in the way of plot. Instead viewers are presented with actions from which they are left to infer meaning. This seems particularly interesting when seen in relation to the wider sociocultural concerns that both pieces appear to surface, suggesting as it does that the work is both in direct conversation with the 'reality' of the world, but also significantly separate from it. It is in the piece *Bliss & Heaven* that the oneiric really emerges. Out of the two pieces we watched in Kiasma, *Bliss & Heaven* was arguably the most fantastical. The somnambulant quality of the overall piece is somewhat at odds with the early moments, in which Just uses editing to impart a sense of incisive and dynamic urgency. In the opening moments, he uses the distinctions between two modes of travel (by foot, by vehicle) to set an initial pace which is slowed down as soon as the younger of the men steals in to the back of the lorry. It is from this moment that the space in between opens up: the absent driver; the absence of light; the absence of a coherent reality as the interior of the truck gives way to the interior of a traditional theatre space, with red velvet curtains pulling back to reveal a further transformation as the formerly 'manly' driver is repositioned through the addition of an acrylic wig and a chiffon scarf. Further gaps open up as he begins to sing: where we might expect the more familiar lip-synching of the drag artist, we are instead treated to his basso profundo, singing Olivia Newton-John's 1978 love song 'Please Don't Keep Me Waiting'. According to Baniotopoulou when writing about the piece:

Please Don't Keep Me Waiting is a classic pop hit and the scene in which it is sung alludes to a real life documentary filmed by Trent Harris in 1979, when he recorded a stranger named Gary perform the song at a talent show in Beaver, Utah, dressed in full drag. Harris restaged the event in 1981 and again in 1985, and put the three parts together to create his 2000 film, *The Beaver Trilogy*. (Baniotopoulou, 2009: unpaginated)

It is in this complex set of relations that a tension arises, allowing for a range of different discourses and articulations to open, some of which are creative, imaginary and personal, as the grasp for a singular reality slips away and alludes us. To further complicate the network of references, the title of *Bliss & Heaven* is taken from Anthony Burgess's *A Clockwork Orange*, from a section of text delivered by the protagonist, Alex.

In the film Just plays with diegetic and non-diegetic sound, using these techniques to undercut the simple realism one might expect. And there is the repeated unfolding of space with the narrative: the unfolding of the field to the truck stop, the back of the truck to a traditional theatre space, the cis-gendered driver to the trans-chanteuse. There are no words in this world; lyrics, yes, but no spoken text. We hear Olivia Newton-John's plea 'Please Don't Keep Me Waiting', but the watchful young man, the 'strapping youth amid sunlit cornfields, wearing dirty jeans and a loose white vest, his hair unkempt' (Barry, 2006) is speechless, confounded by what he sees. This shock seems to come in part from the dislocation of the event at least as much as it does from the event itself. It seems clear that this audience of one is considerably more open and recep-tive to the re-enactment of Newton-John's song than is the case for the original audience he echoes from *The Beaver Trilogy*.

The use of space, its unfolding from the mundane to the bizarre, reveals a relationship between bodies that remains unfolded and unresolved, even as the transformation continues. Quite what transforms is difficult to say: the space between the two men remains unresolved, the distance between the stalls and the stage no less vast than the distance across the corn fields. What has perhaps shifted through is the gaze, with the younger man stepping into the light, proudly owning his position as spectator. In this sense, by stepping into the gaze of the performer, by becoming present in this way, the process of display, ownership and complicity are included in to the conversation. Is this coming into the light, and the concomitant coming into being, a significant moment of queering – not simply because he applauds the trans performer, itself an act which embraces alterity and goes some way to queering the space occupied, but because his body comes into play? Is he waking up, finding his body, his potential for sensual pleasure and moving towards an embodiment? Does the simple act of clapping intro-duce and value the subjective and mark his body? Perhaps as sig-nificant as the text is the casting of Danish actor Johannes Lilleøre (who incidentally plays Karsten Bjerre in series 3 of *Borgen*; the other performer is H. C. Pendersen who also appears in *No Man Is an Island II* (2004) with Lilleøre). Lilleøre, who is cast again and again in eleven of Just's films, functions here as a sort of everyman, involved in this piece (as in many others) in the process of dismantling the fragments of masculinity. Just's returning 'Lilleøre whom the artist thinks of as his alter ego' (Baniotopoulou, 2009: unpaginated) affords Just the opportunity to play out the transformation of this other 'self' across a range of contexts and strategies which court the plausibility of the stereotype.

Both pieces frame their wider concerns through the lens of spectatorship; both use the idea of watching and being watched, the sense of being policed in the performing of one's gender as a means to interrogate masculinity. In many respects, these are pieces about audiencing, about what it is to experience an affective state through performance. And it is through the presence of Lilleøre that we began to make sense of our own spectatorship and the potential for affect that we offered within the work. In both pieces (and arguably in much of Just's other work), there is something explicit about the role of the spectator. In *No Man Is an Island II*, Lilleøre begins as a solo performer, casting all the other men in the bar as audience. Over the course of the short song, each de facto audience member becomes a performer, until there is no one left to perform to. The short film sees communitas develop, a space for radical social interaction where there is a levelling out of behaviours. In Bliss & Heaven it is Lilleøre's willingness to be seen, to go from voyeur to spectator, that gives the piece its potency. Each piece in its own way encourages the audience member to consider our own relationship to looking, a concern that Just interrogates more explicitly in his earlier piece *No Man Is an Island* (2002). In it, Lilleøre presents another moment of spectatorship, but unlike the sense of elation in *Bliss & Heaven*, here he is bereft. The text offers a very different engagement, one that precludes redemption or development for Lilleøre's spectator. Instead, Lilleøre's action is reduced to sitting and crying, with the majority of the framing given over to Niels Weyd, the dancing performer who is thus allowed to own his shambolic physicality and to revel in the sheer joy of movement. His performance of masculinity is in, many ways, less assured than that of the later incarnations of Just's men (the mismatched costume, the public ridicule), but it offers a clearer sense of self and is perhaps less plagued by questions of crisis. The film is much less measured than Just's later work, allowing as it does the accidental to bleed in past the edges of the frame. There is little doubt that the site-specific nature of the display allows space for critique and ridicule from those around him, but it also invites collaboration. His joy becomes infectious, whereas Lilleøre's sadness continues to ensure he remains isolated. Of course Lilleøre's public crying offers a form of resistance of its own, and it is a trope that reappears through much of Just's work.

It is tears, those of Just's performers and those shed in Kiasma, that made us think of Just's work as a means to round out this section. By starting with Baktruppen, and the tears therein, and then finishing here with Just, we have been thinking about a very particular sort of affective transmission. There are inevitable links back to Abramović, but also to other works. The presence of men crying in Just's work evokes work such as Bas Jan Ader's (1971) *I'm Too Sad to Tell You*, or Sam Taylor-Wood's *Crying Men* (2002–2004), which are, on the surface, inevitable analogues with the two pieces of Just's that serve as a coda for this section on affect. We say 'on the surface' deliberately, because in both Ader's and Taylor-Wood's work, the tears are shorn of their signification. Indeed, in Ader's work the title makes explicit that the emotion is too great to be communicated. In Taylor-Wood's work, something else happens; whether deliberately or not, the presence of famous male actors in the images cannot help but remind us as witnesses of Austin's sense that acting is, in his words, infelicitous. It is hard to trust the tears of these men because we know it is their job to feign. Curiously, this was not our response to either Baktruppen or Just's performers, but in both cases there is contextual material to frame the tears, to help them sit within the landscape of communicative affect.

Although the tears that appear in both *No Man Is an Island II* and *Bliss & Heaven* are performed, they are only one part of a larger whole. As Lilleøre is unmanned, a word which speaks so eloquently to the concerns of such work, where the presumed masculine ideals of stoicism and emotional fortitude are interrogated through their absence, we watch from a distance, measuring our own empathy against the distance of the tumbling tears. And it is in this distance that we are able to think about the 'punctum', a small and distinct point explored by Roland Barthes in *Camera Lucida*, and it is across this distance that the onlooker is able to establish a personal connection to the image. But the punctum is also a word that describes wounding, and it is the name of the opening of the tear ducts. When we cry, this first wound opens up. Perhaps it is through the sharing of tears that empathy is born.

Tasks: Affect

How do we leave something? How do we learn to let go, to say farewell?

How do we prepare ourselves to be left? What happens to our bodies, and do we hold ourselves differently in anticipation of the shock of goodbye?

What happens to the places that are full of good-byes? Do the accretions of leaving change how we understand a space?

Dear **[insert name here]**,
I wanted to take a moment to let you know that I am leaving **[insert place here]**. I will be moving on to **[insert other place here]** very soon.

I have really enjoyed/found moderately adequate/thoroughly hated **[delete as appropriate]** my time here and I appreciate having had the opportunity to work with you/talk to you/look at you/ignore you **[delete as appropriate]**. Thank you for the support, guidance, and encouragement/disinterest, avoidance and general lack of engagement **[again, delete as appropriate]** you have provided me during my time at **[insert first place here again]**. Even though I will miss my **[insert random object]**, I am looking forward to this new challenge and to starting a new phase of **[something here]**.

Please keep in touch, or leave me alone, I don't really mind.

Thanks again for everything.

Yours truly,

Lee and Bob x

155

Tasks: Affect

On Affect
The playful nature
of corners

Task instructions
To create an alternate performance geography,
position yourself between two corners. Choose
whether you are performer or spectator, and
wait.

Tasks: Affect

On Affect
Restlessness

> **Task instructions**
> Work on a chair choreography based on ways to settle:
>
> - reconcile yourself into a position
> - decide
> - bring to an end
> - come to terms
> - take up residence and become established
> - become resolved, fixed, established, or quiet
> - come to rest
> - arrange or fix in the desired order
> - dispose of

Tasks: Affect

On Affect

Drawing near

Approach with care

'How do we understand something? We understand something by approaching it. How do we approach something? We approach it from any direction. We approach it using our eyes, our ears, our noses, our intellects, our imaginations. We approach it with silence. We approach it with childhood. We use pain or embarrassment. We use history. We take a safe route or a dangerous one. We discover our approach and we follow it'. (Goulish, 2000, *39 Microlectures in Proximity of Performance*, page 46).

> **Dented knees task**
>
> Where are your 'sore points' in your body, 'sore points' due to theatre? Perhaps a scar from a previous performance, perhaps a muscle that ached from doing the same movement again and again, perhaps something else.
>
> Photograph or draw them. Make into a book and leave it in a hospital/a library/a bus station, because buildings sometimes make us feel better.

Tasks: Affect

On Affect

'Many times my list-making serves as a cure for the ambivalence that pervades a day. It forces a structure or routine upon me when I otherwise would be well satisfied to spend the day gazing in indecisiveness. There is immediate satisfaction from completing the task and crossing it off. I feel I have achieved something [...] They are a justification for existence'.

From Cece Wheeler (2008) 'Listmaking and Other Daily Distractions', *Philament Habits & Habitat*, 12, June (available at http://sydney.edu. au/arts/publications/ philament/issue12_ pdfs/WHEELER_ Listmaking.pdf)

Listing

Love Letter to Barbara, 2006
Joanne 'Bob' Whalley and Lee Miller
24 found shopping lists

In a playful engagement with their local community, Joanne 'Bob' Whalley and Lee Miller collect discarded shopping lists from trolleys outside Waitrose in Kingsthorpe, Northampton, when they go food shopping. She always heads for the shallow trolleys with clipboards. There is some comfort in finding the handwritten scribblings of others, and on those occasions she is lucky enough to find a list they abandon their own dietary wants and needs for those of a stranger's.

Love Letter to Barbara is an open-ended project, which gently engages with an immediate community through the detritus of their everyday existence. The lists themselves serve as a score to Whalley and Miller's shopping trips, providing an alternative to the behaviours and patterns dictated by their weekly shop, and opening up a range of possibilities, leading to the accumulation of things they could not possibly use, in a month of Sundays . . .

> Cigarillos and instant coffee and cat food
> Brillo pads and cheese sauce and line-caught mackerel

After the performed action of shopping, the lists are transformed into origami hearts, acknowledging the affectionate and intimate relationship engaged in with these unknown and unknowing strangers.

> **Task**
> Look for small intimate objects that amuse/interest you, and write them down as a list.

Tasks: Affect

An opening
A hand in close up, some noise coming
from another room, three words whis-
pered with urgency.

A space
Inside, not in the open, not in public, performance arena no more than
3 metres square – maybe it is predetermined or maybe you define your
own limits.

Tasks: Affect

On affect
J'aime response by Chicago performance group Cupola Bobber

'We were asked to make a response to J'aime, a dance performance by Alice Chauchat and Anne Juren, presented at Links Hall in March 2005. This is what we made.

Having been asked to make a response to J'aime, we first asked ourselves what it meant. We thought maybe it would help us if we knew what it meant, but rather than looking it up, we decided to imagine everything it could possibly mean. So what will follow is an absolutely comprehensive list of everything it could mean, we have left nothing out. This unabridged list contains every potential meaning, and leaves none out.

Thank you for this opportunity.

Task

Watch a performance and make an unabridged list that contains every potential meaning, and leaves none out.

J'aime response by Cupola Bobber

1. Dancing
2. Dancing with happiness
3. Dancing with joy
4. Dancing to dance
5. Dancing for fun
6. Dancing to be fun
7. Dancing for you
8. Dancing with me
9. Dancing for or against it
10. Dancing with a sincere amount of embarrassment
11. Dancing with a sincere amount of your gaze
12. Dancing for a sincere gaze
13. Dancing for the possibility of more dancing
14. Dancing without ineptitude
15. Dancing because it's my knees that decide the fate of this here, now
16. Moving, and dancing
17. leaping and dancing
18. Dancing with the possibility of leaping
19. How when I am in a crowd doing the bunny ear dance you look at me and think I am doing the quotes dance.
20. Every Saturday night in 2003
21. The name for when I think I know how you see me.
22. When time becomes Movement
23. The measurement of what constitutes a rave in Chicago. For example: Our j'aimometer is at 25 j'aimes this is no longer a party it has become a rave and must be stopped, everyone must go home.
24. The ingredient that was really at the root of Dance Mania in the 14th and 17th centuries.
25. Your silence amongst the loud unrelenting noise.
26. To Teach by showing.
27. Dressing like a crowd
28. when the pigeons start to sync with the beat on my headphones
29. The combined sound of all creation sung at once
30. To always be in Love
31. The name for the feeling one gets when watching the dancing in the Charlie Brown Christmas Special.
32. Positioning ones self to be looked at.
33. The joy that comes after the terror.
34. Jumping on the bed.
35. Running after spinning while looking at the sky.
36. Looking in to a crowd and seeing myself
37. What my mom thinks about when she thinks about me
38. The time in the car with the stereo on before work
39. The time when the hot soup first hits your lips
40. The best time

41. The time when I thought about you the most
42. In high school, before the prom
43. being scared
44. being really scared
45. being nervous
46. about community
47. about the only thing we do with a lot of strangers
48. about being faceless, but having your eyes closed in a crowd of strangers
49. about bubbles, when they put all the bubbles around you.
50. about a late night call, a really late night and drunken call that makes your stomach hurt in the morning.
51. it
52. then
53. this
54. would
55. could
56. yes
57. yes, and
58. yes
59. it'll be wonderful
60. it'll be perfect
61. it'll be what I've always been looking for
62. it'll be exactly that
63. and tomorrow I'll remember this warmly
64. I'll remember it over coffee
65. I'll wake up slowly, and it'll all come back in a rush
66. how great this was
67. how it was like
68. Dancing
69. Dancing with happiness
70. Dancing with joy
71. Dancing to dance
72. Dancing for fun
73. Dancing to be fun
74. Dancing for you
75. Dancing with me
76. Dancing for or against it
77. Dancing with a sincere amount of embarrassment
78. Dancing with a sincere amount of your gaze
79. Dancing for a sincere gaze
80. Dancing for the possibility of more dancing
81. I'm dancing
82. It's dancing
83. I'm dancing
84. Dancing
85. I'm dancing
86. And you're watching
87. And I'm having fun
88. and I'm dancing.'

('Cupola Bobber', n.d., http://www.cupolabobber.com/projects/jaimeresponse.html)

Tasks: Affect

I want you to find something that makes you angry. Not something small, not plates in the sink, toilets left unflushed, or caps off the toothpaste. No, I mean really angry. Like, so angry, you want to change the world angry.

Find an example of this injustice, and be ready to talk to us all about why you feel the way you do. Oh, and some of you won't be able to do this task. Some of you will encounter your own apathy. Don't run away from that. Spend time asking why.

Tasks: Affect

On affect
an invitation to
tumble

Is there a time-worn place/space that you feel particular affection towards? Do you have an inside of a particular drawer that you would like to open, or a dusty corner you would like more eyes to cast over, or perhaps a favourite tattered chair that gives a certain view of a certain scape?

> **Invitation**
> Introduce new audiences to your chosen place/space.

Tasks: Affect

Place your body somewhere it has never been, and document its new location. How does your presence change the space and the behaviours of the space? What does your presence do to those other people using the space alongside you? Slowly allow the space to shift your behaviours. Use these subtle shifts to generate a new sensitivity. Listen in to yourself. What do you notice? What is missing from this place, and what would you want to introduce? Create a five-minute response, and repeat every day for a week.

Tasks: Affect

How far can sound travel in each space, in a shout or in a whisper?

Tasks: Affect

So, we have a friend, who has this sister. At dinner parties when she is surrounded by conversation that bores her, she takes out a pristine white business card engraved with just two words in small writing. These words read: 'Stop Talking.'

Carry a set of business cards to make others aware of the different emotions you are feeling in any given moment.

Tasks: Affect

Create a **local** smellscape in a box.

In terms of smell, what are the components of the character of a particular place? Send or give it to a friend with instructions of when and where to open the box.

Transport your audience of one through space and time.

> [S]mell is usually associated with the instincts and emotions rather than with reason or spirituality. With few exceptions, smell and smells have been discredited and removed from the arena of intellectual discourse, and, in many cases, from cultural life in general. (Classen, 1998: 36)

Tasks: Affect

Proxemic awareness
Always know how many paces it is between you and your audience. You will need to know how to close that distance, or widen it.

Inch closer. Or perhaps centimetre closer. Now, how does this feel? How close before you feel the warmth emanating from their collective bodies? When does close become too close?

Tasks: Affect

A Task from Dave

Listen to the voices that punctuate the air in supermarkets, airports, train stations. There's something delightful about words spoken over a tannoy system; they are without form, without bodies.

Draw the faces of what you imagine these people look like. Try to find them in person.

Tasks: Affect

There is something unsettling about beginnings – they speak of many things. Beginnings are the things from which I am expected to build my future. And that is where the really hard work happens, because soon you have sailed out of the beginning, and you are somewhere in the middle – that big stretch that is so difficult to fill. The middle is the thing my friend says you will be forgiven for if you start well and end with a flourish. But what might be true of performance is never true in life. The middle is quite possibly the thing that defines you, that allows people to understand the context in which you function. And it is the middle that I find myself contemplating in this moment.

These are the places between A and B, the places that you would probably like to forget.

To celebrate these in-between places take someone – a friend, a relative, a stranger – on a tour of all your favourite places so far.

Tasks: Affect

they occur in the interstices

here are some double
articulations

causing him to be immersed
in a state of flow

engaging her in a disjuncture

a geography of thought
which is folded over and over

n-fold thoughtfulness

Various sites of meeting

they are displayed in tentative
and situated knowledges

Where the boundaries of the
found text is eroded by their
created text

thus allowing for the gaps

Closing

As we discussed earlier, in his book *Thirdspace: Journeys to Los Angeles and other Real-and-Imagined Places*, the cultural geographer Edward Soja argues that space is as important as history and society and that '[t]he spatial dimension of our lives has never been of greater practical and political relevance than it is today' (Soja, 1996: 1). We hope that this book has opened up a space between audience and performer, and applied a wedge/a deviation/a sorbet/a smear/a spanner in the works. The perceptions of space between audience and performer are constructs, and as Winfried Fluck states, boundaries between imagined and real places become blurred: 'in order to gain cultural meaning, physical space has to become mental space, more precisely, imaginary space' (Fluck, 2004: 15). This shift from the actual and 'real' space of audiences into a blurring is the place we are interested in, where we centimetre our way forward towards meaning.

Being practitioner-as-researchers, we constantly ask ourselves what can knowledge 'do', being both aware of how performance might bring about and respond to paradigmatic shifts, but also to take care and hold close to the temporary knowledges which might occur through, around and because of performance practice. Robert Cozzolino, curator at Modern Art, The Pennsylvania Academy of the Fine Arts, created a list of 90-odd statements of intent which begin 'Curator as ...'. Cozzolino explains:

> My family has always been a little baffled by what I do; there have been illuminating moments at exhibition openings and formal talks, but I think they still have very little sense of what a curator does. That's fine, because young and beginning curators also have very little sense of the range of things a curator will be expected to do during his or her run in the field. (Cozzolino, n.d.: unpaginated)

We, like Cozzolino, feel that sometimes bafflement can occur when thinking about the roles of things, and have wondered through these pages about what being an 'audience' might mean and what our role might be within that understanding, both with and through bodies that perform and watch. Cozzolino calls his list 'Job Description: Part 1', and whilst the 'job' of the audience might be easily applied to tick boxes of 'essential' and 'desirable', the burden, or weight, of 'meeting' performance is a responsibility that we wanted take on. Inspired by Cozzolino, below is a final attempt to respond to the increasing complications and complexities of an 'audience', responding to its mercurial qualities to acknowledge these 'chimerical or hydra-headed beasts' (Cozzolino, n.d.: unpaginated),

In noticing its form, listing has always appealed to us as both a structure and a device, but also as a physical manifestation. As we come to an end of this writing, our bodies' baseline state feels like a stricken vessel taking in more than it can possibly cope with. So here we are, listing badly, because to see the world upright would seem like a betrayal. Please feel free to substitute the word 'audience' for something which feels more appropriate, either broadly or for specific interaction. And like Cozzolino, we think this is the closest we have come to describing what we do as/in/to an audience.

Audience as affinity
Audience as artefact
Audience as benevolent
Audience as beside oneself
Audience as brand
Audience as bricklayer
Audience as capsized
Audience as centrifuge
Audience as co-conspirator
Audience as correspondence
Audience as consciousness
Audience as dauntless
Audience as death
Audience as deliberate
Audience as discomposed
Audience as dogs
Audience as drunk
Audience as empathy
Audience as erasure
Audience as erroneous
Audience as final destination

Audience as food
Audience as forgotten
Audience as game
Audience as gorgeous
Audience as healthcare practitioner
Audience as heroes
Audience as honorific
Audience as hot water
Audience as hurt
Audience as immortal
Audience as inky
Audience as interface
Audience as interstice
Audience as irriguous
Audience as jam
Audience as jockey
Audience as karma
Audience as keeping up with the joneses
Audience as kingpin
Audience as knee-trembler
Audience as lacking
Audience as leech
Audience as looming
Audience as lovely
Audience as lungs
Audience as maggot
Audience as meat
Audience as moil
Audience as muscle
Audience as monolithic
Audience as network
Audience as night
Audience as noise
Audience as number
Audience as option
Audience as pea soup
Audience as postcode
Audience as pother
Audience as precise

Audience as quarrel
Audience as quarry
Audience as queer
Audience as questionable
Audience as rapture
Audience as reader
Audience as ready reckoner
Audience as recipe
Audience as religion
Audience as salvo
Audience as smoke
Audience as solicitor
Audience as spaghetti junction
Audience as sparkle
Audience as spoon
Audience as tainted
Audience as teeth
Audience as trouble
Audience as unfit
Audience as undone
Audience as unsound
Audience as vague
Audience as veil
Audience as vigilant
Audience as vomit
Audience as warped
Audience as wary
Audience as weaver
Audience as whimper
Audience as withdrawn
Audience as would-be lover
Audience as wound
Audience as x marks the spot
Audience as X-wings
Audience as X-ray
Audience as yearning
Audience as years
Audience as yeast
Audience as yin and yang
Audience as zeitgeist

Audience as zero
Audience as zombie.

* * *

We started with a story, a story about a tiger, a referee and a cheerleader.

We would like to end with a story, a story about two people tied to chairs whilst having water and talcum powder thrown at them.

With the exception of the brief discussion of the film work of Jesper Just, the performance material we have engaged with has involved live performers being met by live spectators. Although Just's work differs in that the material was mediated, it too focused on questions of spectatorship, with the pieces being presented in a gallery space with spectators sharing the same physical space in the reception of the work. In contrast, this final story focuses entirely upon absence, distance and memory.

During January 2010, Plymouth Arts Centre hosted *The Pigs of Today Are the Hams of Tomorrow*, a weekend-long event bringing together a range of performance arts practices, and a three-day symposium discussing the work. As part of the event, the Performance Re-enactment Society, in collaboration with photographer Hugo Glendinning, created a small studio space in which participants were invited to recreate significant moments of performance. This was a process by which the performer(s), the photographer and members of the re-enactment society would jointly 'own' the moment being restaged. Through the use of a 'flashbulb' memory, these re-enactments opened up questions about ownership and where performance resides once it has been shared with an audience.

Our moment was the 'Drug Trip Scene' from Forced Entertainment's *Club of No Regrets*. I want to say that this was the first piece of performance we had gone to see together, but I'm not sure that is true. Bob had been to see *Emmanuelle Enchanted* the year before, and I knew she was off to see them again, but the company wasn't really on my radar. As I was walking home, I saw the minibus she was travelling in, pulling out of the campus. I raised my hand to wave, and Bob called me over. The side door slid open and she pulled me in, saying that there was a spare ticket and I should definitely go with her. So I did.

It was 1993, and we were in a mini-bus being driven by a guy called Andy. I didn't know where we were heading; in fact, I still don't know where we saw the show, but I do remember the journey home. I was sat on the back seat, looking down the length of the mini-bus, out of the windscreen, Bob was asleep; most people in the bus were. Andy was singing a Queen song, and his attention wasn't fully on the road. I remember shouting to him, 'Andy, is that a pig in the road?', and then there was a big bump as we ran over something. Everyone woke up. We pulled over, got out and went back to see what we'd hit. Turns out I was nearly right. In fact I was exactly half right. We had run over half a pig, sawn down the middle from snout to tail. Strangely, this felt like a perfectly appropriate end to the night. Seeing Forced Entertainment for the first time made finding half a pig in the road feel normal, like it was something that was supposed to happen.

Seventeen years later, we are standing at an event with a pig in the title, an event staged at a former naval victualling yard – a place overlooking the Atlantic, a place that once housed a cooperage, an abattoir, all the things you would expect to keep a navy fed. Over a long, cold weekend in January, in a space that had been taken over by a number of performance artists, we had witnessed a vast array of practices over a short duration. By the time we made our way to meet with the Performance Re-enactment Society, our heads were full of all the practices we had seen over the days, the weeks, the months and years before. And yet it took us no time to alight upon the one moment we would want to re-enact.

As I looked at Lee, I knew exactly the moment we would re-perform; it was a moment we had recreated many times over our years together. If one of us was cooking, and the flour was out of the cupboard, it didn't take long for us to grab a handful, throw it in the air and shout, *'The Drug Trip Scene!'* In fact, we had re-enacted this moment so often, by the time we sat down to re-perform the moment for camera, we were no longer sure what had really happened in the piece. It had taken on a totemic significance in the 'creation myth' of our life together, a joke played out over and over again.

But when it came to performing it under the gaze of Glendinning, the photographer that Forced Entertainment had used for much of its own documentation, we became anxious. Did we know how it looked? What exactly happened? We knew that 'Helen X' had kidnapped two people and made them perform for her, and we knew they were tied to chairs. Or gaffer-taped – maybe they were gaffer-taped to chairs. Once the context had been offered, and we had been tied to our chairs, members of the Performance Re-enactment Society began to throw talc and water at us. And we started to laugh. And laugh. And laugh. Until eventually we had to be reminded that this wasn't a game and that we were supposed to be committing a remembered moment of performance to the archive.

Eventually we stopped laughing, and the photograph was taken. It hangs on the wall of our bedroom. It's the only picture of the two of us we have in the house.

Maybe it's there because it crystallises our concerns about the space between the performer and the audience, because it typifies how one moment can be carried in the body, carried far beyond the moment in which it is experienced, like a leaf on the wind.

Or maybe it's just a really good picture.

Coda

There was this one time that we made a performance in Helsinki.

It was a durational piece installed in the large open foyer space of the Theatre Academy. It lasted for fourteen hours. We called the piece *Into the Good Night (Go)*, and it was our attempt to think about impermanence and loss.

It started at 8 a.m., with Bob writing on Lee's torso the following six words:

'And you have changed my heart.'

She wrote these words with a Sharpie, one of Bob's favourite types of pen. Once these words were written, Lee lay down on a table, and a tattooist called Scotty made these words permanent.

Except of course he didn't. He may have etched the words onto Lee's skin, but they are far from permanent. One day Lee will be dead, and the skin will slide from his bones. The words will vanish, and so too will the person who wrote them.

There was this other time that we made a performance in an abandoned shop in Liverpool. In its own way, this too was a piece about impermanence and loss. The shop we inhabited was due for demolition, part of the regeneration of the city centre. We spent three days living in the shop, each night making a series of small performances in the window. The piece, *Re: Incident On and Off*, started on Friday, and finished on Sunday. Early in the hours of Saturday morning, three men, high on ketamine, broke into the shop. They broke in because they didn't think we were making cake quickly enough.

In both pieces, the audience move into a direct contact with the work, whether as a witness to something that will abide beyond the moment of the performance, or through the insistence that their presence could transgress the normal boundaries of what is and isn't 'appropriate'. As makers, we have been concerned with work that tries its best to dissolve borders. We know that this might result in material that doesn't look too familiar or perhaps leaves the audience uncertain about what exactly their role should be. Our work has tended to focus on these relationships and has worked to keep them in flux.

By now, you have certainly realised that these are also the types of performance we tend to gravitate towards as an audience. We like to step towards work which seems to require something of us; to ask us to meet the work halfway.

And so, we have come to realise that any text we offer to a reader which explores the in-between space of audience and performers should be something that is equally in a state of flux, one which continues to be negotiated through time. As such we consider this writing to a be a venture in process, an undertaking which is delighted to be framed as a beta experience. In theatrical terms, we might call it a 'scratch'. Certainly it is a thing unfolding.

Like those men in Liverpool, and the people craning their necks to watch the tattoo needles scratch at the skin, we would like to invite you to step in. Come a little closer.

Closer.

All of the sections in this book, those which provide nesting space for the theoretical, the analytical, space for stories and for scores, are open and welcome to critique. We started by telling you that this is not a 'how-to' book, that we don't offer the work in here as definitive in any way. With this in mind, we would like to encourage your contributions – we'd like you to augment this text with your own blood, sweat and tears.

And if you wouldn't mind, we'd like to hear about them. We invite you to contact us with your thoughts/additions/donations/frustrations/helping hands:

info@dogshelf.com

Thank you.

Dear Reader...
Thank you

This card is intentionally blank

This card is intentionally blank

This card is intentionally blank

This card is intentionally blank

This card is intentionally blank

This card is intentionally blank

This card is intentionally blank

This card is intentionally blank

This card is intentionally blank

This card is intentionally blank

Bibliography

11 Rooms (2011) durational performance art, curated by Hans Ulrich Obrist and Klaus Biesenbach, Manchester Art Gallery, Manchester International Festival, 9–16 July.

Abramović, Marina (1974) *Rhythm 0*, durational performance art, Studio Morra, Naples.

Abramović, Marina (2009) *Marina Abramović Presents*, durational performance art, Whitworth Art Gallery, Manchester International Festival, 3–17 July.

Abramović, Marina (2010) *The Artist Is Present*, durational performance art, curated by Klaus Biesenbach, Museum of Modern Art (MoMA), New York, 14 March–31 May.

Abramović, Marina (2014) *512 Hours*, durational performance art, Serpentine Gallery, London, 4 June–25 August.

Abramović, Marina and Ulay (1981–1987) *Nightsea Crossing*, durational performance art, numerous sites.

Adler, Janet (2002) *Offering from the Conscious Body: The Discipline of Authentic Movement* (Rochester: Inner Traditions).

Ader, Bas Jan (1971) *I'm Too Sad to Tell You*, art film.

Ahmed, Sara (2014) *The Cultural Politics of Emotion*, 2nd edn (Edinburgh: Edinburgh University Press).

Alston, Adam (2012) 'Funding, Product Placement and Drunkenness in Punchdrunk's *The Black Diamond*, *Studies in Theatre and Performance*, 32(2): 193–208.

Alston, Adam (2013a) 'Politics in the Dark: Risk Perception, Affect and Emotion in Lundahl and Seitl's *Rotating in a Room of Images*', in Nicola Shaughnessy (ed.) *Affective Performance and Cognitive Science: Body, Brain and Being* (London: Methuen).

Alston, Adam (2013b) 'Audience Participation and Neoliberal Value: Risk, Agency and Responsibility in Immersive Theatre', *Performance Research: A Journal of the Performing Arts*, 18(2): 128–38.

Andersson, Danjel (2009) 'A Dream of Baktruppen', in *Performance Art by Baktruppen First Part*, Knut Ove Arntzen and Camilla Eeg-Tverbakk (eds) (Oslo: Kontur Forlag), pp. 15–26.

Arntzen, Knut Ove and Camilla Eeg-Tverbakk (eds) (2009) *Performance Art by Baktruppen First Part*, Oslo: Kontur Forlag.

Arts Council England (2014) 'Hard Facts to Swallow', National Investment Plans 2015–18 Analysis, Commentary and Evaluation, GPS Culture, 10 October, available at http://static.guim.co.uk/ni/1412872263674/GPS-Hard-Facts-to-Swallow-R.pdf.

Auslander, Philip (1999) *Liveness: Performance in a Mediatized Culture* (London: Routledge).

Austin, J. L. (1963) 'How to Do Things with Words', in J. O. Urmson (ed.) *The William James Lectures delivered in Harvard University in 1955* (London: Oxford University Press).

Baktruppen (1999) *Spect*, devised performance, Museum for Contemporary Art, Oslo.

Baktruppen (2004) *Do&Undo*, devised performance, Bowen West Theatre, Bedford, 23 October.

Baktruppen (2007a) 'It Doesn't Workshop Dartington', intensive workshops at Dartington College of Arts, Devon, 5–9 November.

Baktruppen (2007b) '*Do&Undo* Performance Lecture', lecture, Dartington College of Arts, Devon, 5 November.

Baniotopoulou, Evi (2009) 'Jesper Just: Bliss and Heaven (2004)', summary, March, available at http://www.tate.org.uk/art/artworks/just-bliss-and-heaven-t12164/text-summary, unpaginated.

Barry, Hannah (2006) Jesper Just, April 20, available at http://www.jesperjust.com/writings.html.

Barthes, Roland (1970) *S/Z* (Paris: Editions du Seuil).

Barthes, Roland (1982) *Camera Lucida: Reflections on Photography*, trans. by Richard Howard (New York City: Hill and Wang).

Bauer, Otmar (1968) Zeigt [Vomit-Action], colour film of Viennese Actionist performance, 5 minutes.

Beaver Trilogy, The (2001) documentary film, directed by Trent Harris.

Bennett, Susan (1990) *Theatre Audiences: A Theory of Production and Perception* (London and New York: Routledge).

Bentham, Jeremy (2009 [1791]) *Panopticon Or the Inspection House*, Vol. 1 (Whitefish, Montana: Kessinger).

Bishop, Claire (2005) 'No Pictures, Please: The Art of Tino Sehgal', *Artforum International*, 43(9), May, unpaginated, available at http://www.thefreelibrary.com/No+pictures,+please%3A+Clair%20e+Bishop+on+the+art+of+Tino+Sehgal.-a0132554959.

Bishop, Claire (2012) *Artificial Hells: Participatory Art and the Politics of Spectatorship* (London and New York: Verso).

Blade Runner (1982), film, directed by Ridley Scott, written by Hampton Fancher and David Webb Peoples.

Blau, Herbert (1982) *Take Up the Bodies: Theater at the Vanishing Point* (Urbana: University of Illinois Press).

Boal, Augusto (1973/2008) *Theatre of the Oppressed*, translated by Charles A. and Maria-Odilia Leal McBride and Emily Fryer (London: Pluto Press).

Boal, Augusto (1992/2002) *Games for Actors and Non-Actors*, 2nd edn, trans. by Adrian Jackson (London and New York: Routledge).

Bollas, Christopher (1987) *The Shadow of the Object: Psychoanalysis of the Unthought Known* (London: Free Association Books).

Borgen (2010) Danish political drama television, created by Adam Price, written by Adam Price, Jeppe Gjervig Gram and Tobias Lindholm.

Budak, Adam (2005) 'Future Greats', *ArtReview*, 9, December.

Bourdieu, Pierre (1994 [1984]) *Distinction: A Social Critique of the Judgement of Taste*, trans. by Richard Nice (London: Routledge).

Bourgeois, Louise (2002) 'Untitled', score, DO IT at e-flux, available at http://www.e-flux.com/projects/do_it/manuals/0_manual.html.

Breakfast Club, The (1985) film, written, produced, and directed by John Hughes.

Brennan, Teresa (2004) *The Transmission of Affect* (Ithaca and London: Cornell University Press).

Buber, Martin (2010[1937]) *I and Thou* (Eastford, CT: Martino Publishing).

Burgess, Anthony (1995[1962]) *A Clockwork Orange*, New York: W. W. Norton).

Carlson, Marvin (1989) *Places of Performance: The Semiotics of Theatre Architecture* (Ithaca and London: Cornell University Press).

Carlson, Marvin (1996) *Performance: A Critical Introduction*, 2nd edn (London and New York: Routledge.

Chalmers, David (1996) The Conscious Mind: In Search of a Fundamental Theory, Oxford: Oxford University Press).

Charmaz, Kathy (2000) 'Grounded Theory: Objectivist and Constructivist Methods', in Norman K. Denzin and Yvonna S. Lincoln (eds) *Handbook of Qualitative Research*, 2nd edn (Thousand Oaks, CA: Sage), pp. 509–35.

Chatzichristodoulou, Maria and Rachel Zerihan (eds) (2012) *Intimacy Across Visceral and Digital Performance* (Basingstoke: Palgrave MacMillan).

Clark, Robert (2015) *Promise of Happiness*, dance-theatre performance, The Place, 15 May.

Constance Classen (1998) *The Color of Angels: Cosmology, Gender and the Aesthetic Imagination* (London and New York: Routledge).

Connor, Steven and Mirjam Schaub (2015) 'Focus and Echo 4', discussion with Steven Connor and Mirjam Schaub, chaired by Ute Thon, in Ekkehard Skoruppa, Marie-Luise Goerke, Gaby Hartel and Hans Sarkowicz (eds) *Choreographie des Klangs: Zwischen Abstraktion und Erzählung [Choreography of Sound: Between Abstraction and Narration]* (Göttingen and Bristol, CT: Vandenhoeck and Ruprecht), p. 279.

Cozzolino Robert (n.d.) 'Job Description (part one)', originally part of lecture 'Hydra, Juggler, Curator: Reflections on Curatorial Practice' at the Pennsylvania Academy of the Fine Arts, available at http://artjaw. com/robert-cozzolino.

Crossley, Nick (1996) *Intersubjectivity: The Fabric of Social Becoming* (London: Sage).

Cupola Bobber (n.d.) 'j'aime response', performance text, available at http://www.cupolabobber.com/jaimeresponse.html.

Damasio, Antonio (2006) *Descartes' Error* (London: Vintage Books).

Deacon, Robin (2009) 'Are They Really Norwegian?', in Knut Ove Arntzen and Camilla Eeg-Tverbakk (eds) *Performance Art by Baktruppen First Part* (Oslo: Kontur Forlag), pp. 119–34.

Deleuze, Gilles and Félix Guattari (1988) *A Thousand Plateaus: Capitalism and Schizophrenia*, trans. by Brian Massumi (London: The Athlone Press).

Deller, Jeremy (2001) *The Battle of Orgreave*, multi-mode artwork, site-specific performance re-enactment, exhibition, film, and bookwork.

De Marinis, Marco (1987) 'Dramaturgy of the Spectator', *Drama Review*, 31(2), Summer: 100–14.

Dennett, Daniel (1988) 'Quining Qualia', in Anthony J. Marcel and E. Bisiach (eds) *Consciousness in Contemporary Science* (Oxford: Oxford University Press).

Dennett, Daniel (2005) *Sweet Dreams: Philosophical Obstacles to a Science of Consciousness* (London: MIT Press).

Derrida, Jacques (1994) *Specters of Marx: The State of the Debt, the Work of Mourning and the New International*, trans. by Peggy Kamuf (New York and London: Routledge).

Derrida, Jacques (2002 [1972]) *Positions*, trans. by Alan Bass, (London and New York: Continuum).

Diamond, Elin (ed.) (1996) *Performance and Cultural Politics* (London and New York: Routledge).

Dick, Philip K. (1968) *Do Androids Dream of Electric Sheep?* (New York: Doubleday)

Dolan, Jill (1993) 'Geographies of Learning: Theatre Studies, Performance, and the 'Performative'', *Theatre Journal*, 45(4): 417–43.

Dolven, A. K., Tino Sehgal, Steven Connor and Brigitte Felderer (2015) 'Visual Arts: Images Only', panel discussion, chaired by Ute Thon, in Ekkehard Skoruppa, Marie-Luise Goerke, Gaby Hartel and Hans Sarkowicz (eds) *Choreographie des Klangs: Zwischen Abstraktion und*

Erzählung [Choreography of Sound: Between Abstraction and Narration (Göttingen and Bristol, Connecticut: Vandenhoeck and Ruprecht), pp. 303–13.

Duchamp, Marcel (1983) *Notes*, edited by Paul Matisse (Boston: G. K. Hall).

Eldridge, Richard (2001) *The Persistence of Romanticism: Essays in Philosophy and Literature* (Cambridge: Cambridge University Press).

Elias, Amy J. (2011) 'The Narrativity of Post-Convergent Media: No Ghost Just a Shell and Rirkrit Tiravanija's "(ghost reader C.H.)"', *SubStance*, 40(1): 182–202.

Eno, Brian and Peter Schmidt (1975) *Oblique Strategies: Over One Hundred Worthwhile Dilemmas*, limited edition deck of 500 cards, London; revised and reissued, 1978, 1979.

Fensham, Rachel (2009) *To Watch Theatre: Essays on Genre and Corporeality* (Brussels: Peter Lang).

Fluck, Winfried (2004) 'Theories and Methods. Imaginary Space; or, Space as Aestethic Object', in Lother Hönnighausen, Julia Apitzsch and Wibke Rege (eds) *Space – Place – Environment* (Stauffenburg Verlag).

Forbes, Bici (1966) 'Becoming Invisible', score published in Ken Friedman, Owen Smith and Lauren Sawchyn (eds) special 2002 edition of *Fluxus Performance Workbook*, digital supplement to *Performance Research*, 7(3), 'On Fluxus', September 2002, (London: Routledge/Taylor & Francis).

Freshwater, Helen (2009) *Theatre and Audience* (Basingstoke: Palgrave MacMillan).

Friday Night Lights (2006–11) US television drama, developed by Peter Berg, executive produced by Brian Grazer, David Nevins, Sarah Aubrey and Jason Katims, aired on NBC and The 101 Network.

Gaga, Lady and Millie Brown (2014) *Swine*, performance, SXSW Music Festival, Texas, 14 March.

Gardiner, Michael (1992) 'Bakhtin's Carnival: Utopia as Critique', *Utopian Studies*, 3(2): 21–49.

Geertz, Clifford (1973) *The Interpretation of Cultures: Selected Essays* (New York: Basic Books).

Gendlin, Eugene (2007) *Focussing* (New York: Bantam Dell).

Ghost in the Shell (1995) animated film, directed by Mamoru Oshii, written by Kazunori Itō.

Giannachi, Gabriella, Nick Kaye and Michael Shanks (eds) (2012) *Archaeologies of Presence: Art Performance and the Persistence of Being* (London and New York: Routledge).

Ginters, Laura (2010) 'On Audiencing: The Work of the Spectator in Live Performance', *About Performance*, 10: 7–14.

Goffman, Erving (1990 [1959]) *The Presentation of Self in Everyday Life* (London: Penguin Books).

Goldberg, RoseLee (1979) *Performance: Live Art 1909 to the Present* (London: Thames and Hudson).

Goldberg, RoseLee (1998) *Performance: Live Art Since the 60's*, foreword by Laurie Anderson (London: Thames and Hudson).

Goldberg, RoseLee (2001) *Performance Art: From Futurism to the Present*, revised and expanded edition (London: Thames and Hudson).

Gordon, Christopher, David Powell and Peter Stark (2014) 'Regional Arts Funding Imbalance Will 'Worsen Significantly', Warns Arts Leaders', *The Guardian*, 10 October, available at http://www.theguardian.com/culture-professionals-network/culture-professionals-blog/2014/oct/10/arts-funding-imbalance-hard-facts-report.

Goulish, Matthew (2000) *39 Microlectures: In Proximity of Performance* (London and New York: Routledge).

Grehan, Helen (2009) *Performance, Ethics and Spectatorship in a Global Age* (Basingstoke: Palgrave Macmillan).

Griffin, Tim (2005) 'Tino Sehgal: An Interview', *Artforum International*, 43, May, unpaginated, available at http://www.thefreelibrary.com/Tino+Sehgal+an+interview.-a0132554960.

Hall, Edward T. (1990[1966]) *The Hidden Dimension* (New York and Toronto: Anchor Books).

Heathfield, Adrian and Amelia Jones (eds) (2012) *Perform, Repeat, Record: Live Art in History* (Chicago: University of Chicago Press).

Heidegger, Martin (1971) *Poetry, Language, Thought*, trans. by Albert Hofstadter (New York: Harper and Row).

Hill, Leslie and Helen Paris (2014) *Performing Proximity: Curious Intimacies* (Basingstoke: Palgrave MacMillan).

Hilton, Julian (1988) *Performance, New Directions in Theatre* (Basingstoke: Palgrave MacMillan).

Holmberg, Arthur (1996) *The Theatre of Robert Wilson* (Cambridge: Cambridge University Press).

Horton, Donald and Richard Wohl (1956) 'Mass Communication and Para-social Interaction: Observations on Intimacy at a Distance', *Psychiatry: Interpersonal and Biological Processes*, 19(3): 1956.

Hsieh, Tehching (2008) One Year Performance 1981–1982, statement, available at http://www.tehchinghsieh.com.

Hsieh, Tehching and Adrian Heathfield (2015) *Out of Now: The Life-works of Tehching Hsieh*, updated edition (Chicago: University of Chicago Press).

Hu, Tung-Hui (2015) *A Prehistory of the Cloud* (Massachusetts and London: The MIT Press).

Huyghe, Pierre and Philipe Parreno (2002) *No Ghost, Just a Shell*, installed at the Kunsthalle, Zürich, 24 August–27 October 2002.

Irigaray, Luce (1985) *This Sex Which Is Not One*, trans. by Catherine Porter with Carolyn Burke (Ithaca, New York: Cornell University Press).

Jones, Amelia and Andrew Stephenson (eds) (1999) *Performing the Body/ Performing the Text* (London and New York, Routledge).

Just, Jesper (2004) *No Man Is an Island II*, art film, viewed at Kiasma Museum of Contemporary Art, Helsinki, Finland.

Just, Jesper (2004) *Bliss & Heaven*, art film, viewed at Kiasma Museum of Contemporary Art, Helsinki, Finland.

Kaprow, Allan (1959) *18 Happenings in 6 Parts*, performance, Reuben Gallery, New York.

Kennedy, Dennis (2009) *The Spectator and the Spectacle: Audiences in Modernity and Post-modernity* (Cambridge: Cambridge University Press).

Klein, Melanie (1984[1946]) 'Notes on Some Schizoid Mechanisms', in R. E. Money-Kyrle et al., *The Writings of Melanie Klein* (London: Hogarth).

Koskinen, Ilpo, John Zimerman, Thomas Binder, Johan Redström, and Stephan Wensveen (2011) *Design Research Through Practice: From The Lab, Field, and Showroom* (Amsterdam: Elsevier).

Kosofsky Sedgwick, Eve (2003) *Touching Feeling: Affect, Pedagogy, Performativity* (Durham, NC: Duke University Press).

Laird, J. D. (1974) 'Self-attribution of Emotion: The Effects of Expressive Behavior on the Quality of Emotional Experience', *Journal of Personality and Social Psychology*, 29, April 1974: 475–86.

Machonn, Josephine (2013) *Immersive Theatres: Intimacy and Immediacy in Contemporary Performance* (Basingstoke: Palgrave MacMillan).

Marranca, Bonnie (2003) 'The Wooster Group: A Dictionary of Ideas', *PAJ: A Journal of Performance and Art*, 25 (2), May: 1–18.

Massumi, Brian (2010) 'The Political Ontology of Threat', in Melissa Gregg and Gregory J. Seigworth (eds) *The Affect Theory Reader* (London: Duke University Press).

Massumi, Brian (2015) *Politics of Affect* (Cambridge: Polity Press).

Mayer, Emeran A. (2011) 'Gut Feelings: The Emerging Biology of Gut–Brain Communication', *Nature Reviews Neuroscience*, 12(8): 453–66.

McConachie, Bruce (2008) *Engaging Audiences: A Cognitive Approach to Spectating in the Theatre* (Basingstoke: Palgrave Macmillan).

McConachie, Bruce (2013) *Theatre and Mind* (Basingstoke: Palgrave Macmillan).

McKenzie, Jon (2001) *Perform or Else: From Discipline to Performance* (London and New York: Routledge).

McQuaid, James (2014) 'Audience Engagement in Arts and Heritage: The Traps We Fall Into', *The Guardian*, 6 October, available at http://www.theguardian.com/culture-professionals-network/culture-professionals-blog/2014/oct/06/audience-engagement-arts-heritage-traps.

Michalaka J, K., K. Rohdeb and N .K. Trojec (2015) 'How We Walk Affects What We Remember: Gait Modifications through Biofeedback Change Negative Affective Memory Bias', *Journal of Behavior Therapy and Experimental Psychiatry*, 46, March: 121–25.

Roberta Mock (forthcoming) 'Experiencing Michael Mayhew's Away in a Manger: Spectatorial Immersion in Durational Performance', in James Frieze (ed.) *Reframing Immersive Theatre: The Politics and Pragmatics of Participatory Performance* (Basingstroke: Palgrave Macmillan).

Moehrke, Una H. (2011) 'Another Mode of Production, Ingrid Hentschel, Una H. Moehrke and Klaus Hoffmann (eds) *Tino Sehgal im Gespräch mit Una H. Moehrke, in Im Modus der Gabe [In the Mode of Giving] Theater, Kunst, Performance in der Gegenwart [Theater, Art, Performance in the Present]* (Bielefeld: Kerber Verlag), pp. 116–22.

Morris, Pam (ed.) (1994) *The Bakhtin Reader: Selected Writings of Bakhtin, Medvedev, Voloshinov* (London: Edward Arnold).

Morton, Timothy (2013) Hyperobjects: Philosophy and Ecology after the End of the World (Minneapolis and London: University of Minnesota Press).

Mulvey, Laura (1975) 'Visual Pleasure and Narrative Cinema', *Screen*, 16(3): 6–18.

Museum of Modern Art (MoMA) (2010) Marina Abramović's *The Artist Is Present*, live stream of durational performance art, at MoMA, Museum of Modern Art, New York, 14 March – 31 May, [online] available: http://www.moma.org/interactives/exhibitions/2010/marinaabramovic/.

Newton-John, Olivia (1978) 'Please Don't Keep Me Waiting', song, written by Stephen Sinclair and Joe Falsia.

Nield, Sophie (2008) 'The Rise of the Character Named Spectator', *Backpages Contemporary Theatre Review*, 18(4): 531–44.

Obrist, Hans Ulrich (2003) interview with Tino Seghal, Katalog des Kunstpreises der Böttcherstaße, Bremen, unpaginated, available at http://www.johnengalerie.de/fileadmin/Download/Press/sehgal/Sehgal_Interview_mit_Obrist_2003.pdf.

Oddey, Alison and Christine White (2009) *Modes of Spectating* (Bristol and Chicago: Intellect).

Orbison, Roy (1962) 'Crying', song, written by Roy Orbison and Joe Melson.

Orphan Black (2013 –) TV show, BBC America, created by John Fawcett and Graeme Manson.

Padfield, Deborah and Brian Hurwitz (2003) 'As If . . . Visualizing Pain', photo essay, *International Journal of Epidemiology*, 32: 704–07.

Pallaro, Patrizia (ed.) (1999) *Authentic Movement: Essays by Mary Starks Whitehouse, Janet Adler and Joan Chodorow* (London and Philadelphia: Jessica Kingsley).

Pavis, Patrice (1992) *Theatre at the Crossroads of Culture* (London: Routledge).

Pearson, Mike and Michael Shanks (2001) *Theatre/Archaeology* (London: Routledge).

Perry, John (2012) 'Return of the Zombies?', in Simone Gozzano and Christopher S. Hill (eds) *New Perspectives on Type Identity: The Mental and The Physical* (Cambridge: Cambridge University Press).

Penny, David (2015) *Work on the Line*, handmade edition, June.

Phelan, Peggy (1993) *Unmarked: The Politics of Performance* (London and New York: Routledge).

Phelan, Peggy (2009) 'Dwelling', in Adrian Heathfield (ed.) *Out of Now: The Lifeworks of Tehching Hsieh* (London and Cambridge, MA: Live Art Development Agency and MIT Press).

Plato (1930 [370 B.C.]) *The Republic*, Vol. 1, trans. by Paul Shorey (Cambridge, Massachusetts: Harvard University Press).

Punchdrunk (2013) *The Drowned Man: A Hollywood Fable*, immersive promenade performance, May, 31 London Street, London.

Rancière, Jacques (2007) 'The Emancipated Spectator', *Artforum*, March: 271–80.

Rancière, Jacques (2009) *The Emancipated Spectator*, trans. by Gregory Elliott (London and New York: Verso).

Richards, Mary (2012) 'This Progressive Production: Agency, Durability and Keeping it Contemporary', *Performance Research: A Journal of the Performing Arts*, 15(5): 71–77.

Ricoeur, Paul (1970) *Freud and Philosophy: An Essay on Interpretation* (New Haven: Yale University Press).

Russeth, Andrew (2013) 'Would You Rather Feel Too Busy, or Not Busy Enough?' Tino Sehgal at Marian Goodman's Frieze Booth', *The Observer*, 5 October 2013, available at http://observer.com/2013/05/would-you-rather-feel-too-busy-or-not-busy-enough-tino-sehgal-at-marian-goodmans-frieze-booth.

Schaub, Mirjam (2015) 'Voices, Calling and Performing', keynote, in Ekkehard Skoruppa, Marie-Luise Goerke, Gaby Hartel and Hans Sarkowicz (eds) *Choreographie des Klangs: Zwischen Abstraktion und Erzählung [Choreography of Sound: Between Abstraction and Narration]* (Göttingen and Bristol, CT: Vandenhoeck and Ruprecht), pp. 267–75.

Schechner, Richard (1994 [1973]) *Environmental Theater* (New York: Applause Publications).

Schechner, Richard (2002) *Performance Studies: An Introduction* (London and New York: Routledge).

Schön, Donald A. (1983) *The Reflective Practitioner: How Professionals Think in Action* (New York: Basic Books).

Schneider, Rebecca (2012) 'Performance Remains Again', in Gabriella Giannachi, Nick Kaye, and Michael Shanks (eds) *Archaeologies of Presence: Art, Performance and the Persistence of Being* (London and New York: Routledge), pp. 64–81.

Shakespeare, William (1977) 'Hamlet', in R. R. Young (ed.) *The South Bank Shakespeare* (London: University Tutorial Press).

Simpsons, The (2000) 'Alone Again, Natura-Diddily', US animated sitcom, written by Ian Maxtone-Graham and directed by Jim Reardon, 13 February.

Soja, Edward W. (1996) *Thirdspace: Journeys to Los Angeles and Other Real-and-Imagined Places* (Massachusetts and Oxford: Blackwell).

Soja, Edward W. (2000) 'Thirdspace: Expanding the Scope of the Geographical Imagination', in Alan Read (ed.) *Architecturally Speaking: Practices of Art, Architecture and the Everyday* (London and New York: Routledge), pp. 13–30.

Solnit, Rebecca (2004) *Hope in the Dark: Untold Histories, Wild Possibilities* (New York: Nation Books).

Soyini Madison, D. and Judith Hamera (2005) *The Sage Handbook of Performance Studies* (London: Sage).

Sweet Charity (1969) musical film, directed and choreographed by Bob Fosse, written by Neil Simon, music by Cy Coleman and Dorothy Fields.

Tanke, Joseph J. (2011) *Jacques Rancière : An Introduction* (London and New York: Continuum International).

Tanner, Marcia (2002) 'No Ghost, Just a Shell' review, hosted by Stretcher: Visual Culture in the Bay Area and Beyond, available at http://www.stretcher.org/features/no_ghost_just_a_shell/.

Taylor-Wood, Sam (2002–2004) *Crying Men*, art photography.

Teen Wolf (1985) film, directed by Rod Daniel, written by Jeph Loeb and Matthew Weisman.

Tofts, Darren (2011) 'Fluxus Thirty-Eight Degrees South: An interview with Ken Friedman', *Postmodern Culture*, 2(3), May, available at http://agora8.org/documents/DarrenTofts/.

Transformers 2: Revenge of the Fallen (2009) film, directed by Michael Bay, written by Ehren Kruger, Roberto Orci and Alex Kurtzman.

Triplett, Norman (1898) 'The Dynamogenic Factors in Pacemaking and Competition, *The American Journal of Psychology*, 9(4): 507–33.

Turner, Edith (2012) *Communitas: The Anthropology of Collective Joy* (Basingstoke: Palgrave MacMillan).

Turner, Victor (1969) 'Liminality and Communitas', in Victor Turner, Roger D. Abrahams and Alfred Harris (eds) *The Ritual Process: Structure and Anti-Structure* (Chicago: Aldine Publishing), pp. 94–113.

Tye, Michael (2015) 'Qualia', in *The Stanford Encyclopaedia of Philosophy*, available at http://plato.stanford.edu/entries/qualia/.

Wheeler, Cece (2008) 'Listmaking and other Daily Distractions', *Philament: Habits and Habitat*, 12, June, available at http://sydney.edu.au/arts/publications/philament/issue12_pdfs/WHEELER_Listmaking.pdf.

Welton, Martin (2011) *Feeling Theatre* (Basingstoke: Palgrave MacMillan).

Wesemann, Arnd (2009) 'What Did Baktruppen Actually Do?', in Knut Ove Arntzen and Camilla Eeg-Tverbakk (eds) *Performance Art by Baktruppen First Part* (Oslo: Kontur Forlag), pp. 41–42.

Wetherell, Margaret (2012) *Affect and Emotion: A New Social Science Understanding* (London: Sage).

Whalley, Joanne 'Bob' and Lee Miller (2006) *Barbara*, ongoing performance in supermarkets.

Whalley, Joanne 'Bob' and Lee Miller (2006) *Re: Incident On and Off*, durational site-specific performance, performed as Fictional Dogshelf Theatre Company, Liverpool Biennial, 28–30 October.

Whalley, Joanne 'Bob' and Lee Miller (2013a) *Into The Good Night (Go)*, durational site-specific performance, Theatre Academy, Helsinki, 28 February.

Whalley, Joanne 'Bob' and Lee Miller (2013b) 'Look Right Through: Intention and Accident in Performer/Audience Training', in *Theatre, Dance and Performance Training*, 4(1): 102–12.

White, Gareth (2013) *Audience Participation in Theatre: Aesthetics of the Invitation* (Basingstoke: Palgrave MacMillan).

Whitehouse, Mary (1963) 'Physical Movement and Personality', in Patrizia Pallaro (ed.) *Authentic Movement: Essays by Mary Starks Whitehouse, Janet Adler and Joan Chodorow* (London and Philadelphia: Jessica Kingsley).

Wilson, Robert (2011) *The Life and Death of Marina Abramović*, performed by Marina Abramović, Antony, Willem Dafoe, Manchester International Festival, The Lowry, 9–16 July.

Wittgenstein, Ludwig (1968 [1953]) *Philosophical Investigations*, trans. by G.E.M. Anscombe (Oxford: Basil Blackwell).

Zlatev, Jordan, Tony P. Racine, Chris Sinha and Esa Itkonen (eds) (2008) *The Shared Mind: Perspectives in Intersubjectivity* (Amsterdam and Philadelphia: John Benjamin's).

Index

A

Abramović, Marina   29
  512 Hours (2014)   2
  Marina Abramović Presents
    (2009)   2
  Nightsea Crossing (1981–1987)   2
  The Artist is Present (2010)   2, 3, 4,
    6, 7, 14, 17, 18, 21, 25, 29, 30, 33,
    34, 35, 116, 122
  *The Life and Death of Marina
    Abramović* (2011)   2
  Rhythm 0 (1974)   24
Action Hero
  Hoke's Bluff   vii
Ader, Bas Jan
  I'm Too Sad to Tell You (1971)   154
Adler, Janet   14
affect   ix, x, 2, 16, 19, 21, 35, 61, 63,
    74, 76, 78, 79, 83, 90, 91, 124,
    131–135, 137–139, 142, 146, 148,
    150
  affective states   xiv, 16, 62, 78, 83,
    84, 85, 86, 95, 96, 124, 131, 132,
    133, 139, 144, 145, 149, 153
  affective exchange /
    transmission   76, 78, 91, 96, 122,
    127, 146, 148, 154
  affective turn   16, 131, 142
Ahmed, Sara   119, 132, 144
Alston, Adam   124, 138, 144
Andersson, Danjel   117, 118, 126
Arts Council England   27, 31
audience   ix–xvi, 1, 2, 4, 7–15, 18–33,
    65, 66, 67, 69, 73, 74, 76–78,
    83, 88, 91–96, 117, 118, 120,
    122–126, 129–131, 133, 139, 143,
    144, 146–148, 152, 153, 173–177,
    179–181

audience engagement   2–4, 7, 19,
    21, 24–26, 29, 31–33, 76, 91,
    94–96, 123, 153
audience participation   10–13
audiencing   9, 10, 122, 153
Auslander, Philip   3
Austin, J. L.   82, 83, 135–138, 140,
    141, 146, 154
Authentic Movement   13, 91

B

Baktruppen   116, 117, 119–122, 125,
    126, 154
  Do & Undo (2004)   116, 119, 122
  Spect (1999)   121
Baniotopoulou, Evi   151, 153
Barthes, Roland   x, 23, 154
Bauer, Otmar   34
  Zeigt [Vomit-Action] (1968)   34
Bennett, Susan   10, 14, 26, 27, 31, 32,
    129
Bentham, Jeremy   25
Bishop, Claire   12, 13–16, 65
Blau, Herbert   74
Boal, Augusto   32
Bollas, Christopher   89–91
Borgen   152
Bourdieu, Pierre   27, 51
Bourgeois, Louise   103
  Untitled (2002)   103
Bowen West Theatre, Bedford   116
brain   xv, 80, 84, 86, 87, 90, 138,
    144–146
Breakfast Club, The (1985)   vii
Brennan, Teresa   63, 78, 86, 132–135,
    143, 146, 147
Brown, Millie   34
  Swine (2014)   34

Buber, Martin   94, 127, 128
Budak, Adam   150, 151
Burgess, Anthony   152
   A Clockwork Orange
      (1995[1962])   152

C

Carlson, Marvin   28
Chalmers, David   79, 81
Chatzichristodoulou, Maria   10, 125
Clark, Robert   143, 145
   Promise of Happiness (2015)   143
Cloud, The   71–73, 75, 82
cognition   80, 83, 86, 87
communitas   14, 15, 16, 153
consciousness   15, 79, 80, 83, 85, 86,
      90, 91, 127, 174
Cozzolino, Robert   173, 174
Crossley, Nick   127
cultural capital   27, 31
Cupola Bobber   161, 162
curator
   curation   70
   curatorship   3, 26, 173

D

Damasio, Antonio   83–85, 89, 90, 96,
      138, 139, 146
Dartington College of Arts,
      Devon   120, 121
De Marinis, Marco   22, 23, 26, 27,
      125, 129
Deacon, Robin   121
Deleuze, Gilles   xiv, 94, 95
Deller, Jeremy
   The Battle of Orgreave (2001)   12,
      14–16
   Dennett, Daniel   xiv, xv, 80–83,
      85–87, 90
Derrida, Jacques   121, 137, 140,
      146
devised performance   ix, 83
Diamond, Elin   28
Dick, Philip K.
   *Do Androids Dream of Electric
      Sheep?* (1968)   70
digital performance   43, 60, 62, 177

Dolan, Jill   27, 140
dramaturgy   22
Duchamp, Marcel   78, 79, 134

E

Eldridge, Richard   148
emancipated spectator   11, 23
embodiment   15, 146, 152
emotion   viii, 1, 2, 3, 6, 7, 11, 16, 21,
      35, 63, 81, 82, 83, 84, 90, 116,
      117, 124, 131, 132, 135, 137, 138,
      145, 146, 148, 154, 167, 168
Eno, Brian   xi
environment   20, 26, 56, 62, 93, 109,
      124, 126, 127, 144
ethics   16

F

feeling   viii, 11, 56, 80, 82, 85, 91, 99,
      100, 117, 119, 125, 127, 131–135,
      138–140, 143–147, 167
Fensham, Rachel   10
Fluck, Winfried   173
Fluxus   xi
focusing   91
Forbes, Bici   75
   Become Invisible (1966)   75
Freshwater, Helen   10, 24
Friday Night Lights (2006–2011)   vii

G

Gaga, Lady   34
   Swine (2014)   34
Gardiner, Michael   129
Geertz, Clifford   40
Gendlin, Eugene   91
Mamoru Oshii & Kazunori Itō
   Ghost in the Shell (1995)   60
Giannachi, Gabriella   2
Ginters, Laura   10–12
Goffman, Erving   29, 136
Goldberg, RoseLee   24, 28
Gordon, Christopher   31
Goulish, Matthew   ix, 158
Grehan, Helen   10
Griffin, Tim   65

Guattari, Félix xiv, 94, 95
gut feeling 125, 144, 145

H
Hall, Edward T. 19, 20
Hamera, Judith 82
Harris, Trent 151
  Beaver Trilogy (2001) 151, 152
Heathfield, Adrian 75, 76, 96
Heidegger, Martin 59, 74, 123
Hill, Leslie 10, 19, 20, 58, 125, 133
Hilton, Julian 19, 20
Holmberg, Arthur 103
Horton, Donald 92, 93
Hsieh, Tehching 37
  One Year Performance (1981–
  1982) 37
Hu, Tung-Hui 71
Huyghe, Pierre 60, 70, 82
  No Ghost, Just a Shell (2002) 60

I
immersive theatres 10, 11, 23, 25, 26,
  30, 123, 124, 125, 130, 144
intersubjectivity 5, 6, 19, 61, 76, 77,
  78, 92, 95, 122, 125, 127, 128,
  129, 130, 131, 132, 137, 146
  intersubjective exchange xiii, 8, 18,
  21, 22, 27, 32, 79, 88, 94, 95, 124,
  126, 130, 131, 143
intimacy x, 9, 10, 19, 20, 21, 67, 74,
  90, 92, 93, 94, 126, 127, 130, 133,
  159
Irigaray, Luce 61

J
Jones, Amelia 3
Just, Jesper 148–154, 177
  Bliss & Heaven (2004) 148–154
  No Man Is An Island II
  (2004) 148–150, 153, 154

K
Kaprow, Allan 29
Kaye, Nick 2
Kennedy, Dennis 10

Klein, Melanie 141
Koskinen, Ilpo xi
Kosofsky Sedgwick, Eve 135

L
Laird, J.D. 84
live art 75

M
Manchester Art Gallery 59, 73
Manchester International Festival 2,
  59
Marranca, Bonnie 43
Martin-Gropius-Bau 64–66
Massumi, Brian 16, 131, 132,
  137–139, 146
Mayer, Emeran A. 144–146
Mayhew, Michael 24
McConachie, Bruce 10, 125
McKenzie, Jon 28, 72
McQuaid, James 26–27, 31, 92
Michalaka, J. K. 84
Miller, Lee 24, 35, 81, 159
Mock, Roberta 24
Moehrke, Una H. 66
MoMA, Museum of Modern Art, New
  York 2, 3, 4, 26, 30
Morris, Pam 128
Morton, Timothy 36
Mulvey, Laura 13

N
Newton-John, Olivia 151, 152
  Please Don't Keep Me Waiting
  (1978) 151, 152

O
Obrist, Hans Ulrich 71
Oddey, Alison 10
Orbison, Roy (1962) *Crying* 149
Orphan Black (2013–) 68

P
p-zombie 81–83
Padfield, Deborah 88, 89
panopticon 25

para-social   21, 92–96, 130
Parreno, Philipe   60, 70, 82
  No Ghost, Just a Shell (2002)   60
Paris, Helen   10, 19, 20, 58, 125, 133
participant   10, 13, 15, 36, 96, 177
participatory art   12, 15
Pavis, Patrice   2, 3
Pearson, Mike   40
perception   2, 3, 7, 88, 118, 124, 127,
    128, 173
performance art   ix, 30, 34, 69, 83,
    119, 121, 177, 178
performance studies   x, 28–30, 82,
    124, 129
performative   20, 82, 129, 135–139,
    142, 146
Perry, John   79
Phelan, Peggy   3, 24, 77
Plato   11, 12, 147
postmodern   11
Powell, David   31
proxemics   x, 19, 20, 21, 126, 130,
    133
proximity   19, 20, 21, 127, 158
psychoneuroendocrinology   63, 86,
    134
Punchdrunk   17, 30
  *The Drowned Man: A Hollywood
  Fable* (2013)   29

Q
qualia   ix, x, xiv, 21, 74, 79, 80, 81,
    82, 86–92, 147
  quale   79, 91
  qualic exchange   58, 88, 91, 92,
    94–96

R
Rancière, Jacques   11, 12, 13, 14, 24, 25
ritual   22, 148
Rohdeb, K.   84
Russeth, Andrew   62, 63

S
Schaub, Mirjam   65
Schechner, Richard   4, 22–29, 125,
    129

Schmidt, Peter   xi
Schneider, Rebecca   6, 17, 65, 74
Schön, Donald A.   xii, xiii
Blade Runner (1982)   70
Sehgal, Tino,   59, 60, 64, 65, 70
  Ann Lee   58, 59–62, 63, 64, 66–76,
    81, 82, 92
  Kiss (2007)   66
  This Situation (2007)   67
  This Variation (2012)   66
  Yet Untitled (2013)   67
Serpentine Gallery, London   2
Shanks, Michael   2, 40
Simpsons, The   viii
Soja, Edward W.   72, 73, 87, 173
Solnit, Rebecca   100
Soyini Madison, D.   82
spectactor   32
spectator   ix, xii, xiii, xiv, xv, 2, 3,
    10–15, 18–24, 27, 29, 30, 33, 59,
    60, 63, 64, 66, 68–70, 76–78, 91,
    92, 93, 94, 122, 123, 125, 138,
    147, 148, 152, 153, 156, 177
Stark, Peter   31
Sweet Charity (1969)   1

T
Tanner, Marcia   60, 61
Taylor, Diana   29
Taylor-Wood, Sam
  Crying Men (2002–2004)   154
Teen Wolf (1985)   vii
The Place, London   139
Theatre/Archaeology   40
thirdspace   72, 73
Transformers 2: Revenge of the Fallen
    (2009)   1, 8
transmission   29, 76, 78, 91, 96, 132,
    133, 147, 154
Triplett, Norman   18
Trojec, N.K.   84
Turner, Edith & Victor   14
Tye, Michael   86, 87

U
Ulay
  Nightsea Crossing (1981–1987)   2

W

Welton, Martin   10, 125
Wesemann, Arnd   125
Wetherell, Margaret   138, 139
witness   13–16, 25, 29, 62, 63, 64, 71,
    73, 76, 78, 79, 81, 91, 119, 124,
    125, 128, 146, 154
Whalley, Joanne 'Bob'   24, 35,
    159
Wheeler, Cece   159
White, Christine   10
White, Gareth   10

Whitehouse, Mary   14
Whitworth Art Gallery   2, 8
Wilson, Robert   103, 126
    *The Life and Death of Marina
    Abramović* (2011)   2
Wittgenstein, Ludwig   97
Wohl, Richard   92, 93
Wooster Group, The   43

Z

Zerihan, Rachel   10, 125
Zlatev, Jordan   127, 128